D0858422

YT

BLACK BUSINESS
IN THE BLACK METROPOLIS

Blacks in the Diaspora

Darlene Clark Hine, John McCluskey, Jr. and David Barry Gaspar
General Editors

BLACK BUSINESS IN THE BLACK METROPOLIS

The Chicago Metropolitan
Assurance Company, 1925–1985

ROBERT E. WEEMS, JR.

INDIANA UNIVERSITY PRESS

Bloomington and Indianapolis

Library of Congress Cataloging-in-Publication Data

Weems, Robert E., date
    Black business in the Black metropolis : the Chicago Metropolitan
Assurance Company, 1925–1985 / Robert E. Weems, Jr.
        p.   cm. — (Blacks in the diaspora)
    Includes bibliographical references and index.
    ISBN 0-253-33025-4 (cloth)
    1. Chicago Metropolitan Assurance Company—History. 2. Insurance
companies—Middle West—History. 3. Afro-American business
enterprises—Middle West—History. I. Title. II. Series.
HG8538.M53W43   1996
365´.06´577311—dc20   95-23294

1   2   3   4   5   01   00   99   98   97   96

CONTENTS

Illustrations follow page 76.

LIST OF TABLES

ACKNOWLEDGMENTS

Although historical research is essentially a solitary endeavor, the historian, while working on a project, meets a variety of helpful individuals. Without this support group of funding agencies, librarians, archivists, colleagues, etc., scholarly investigation would grind to a screeching halt. Among the numerous individuals and institutions I am personally indebted to are: the University of Wisconsin-Madison Graduate School's Advanced Opportunity Program; Stanley K. Schultz, my dissertation advisor; Walter B. Weare of the University of Wisconsin-Milwaukee; Perry Duis of the University of Illinois-Chicago; Jim Grossman of the Newberry Library; Mrs. Clarice Hal, former executive director of the National Insurance Association; Juliet E. K. Walker of the University of Illinois-Champaign/Urbana; the Special Collections / Manuscript Departments of the University of Chicago Library, the University of Illinois-Chicago Library, and the Chicago Historical Society; the Vivian Harsh African American History Collection at the Carter G. Woodson Regional Library in Chicago; the National Archives Regional Center in Chicago; the Chicago Urban League's Research Department; and the University of Missouri-Columbia's Summer Research Fellowship Program. A special thanks goes to Indiana University Press, especially to Darlene Clark Hine for her support of this project.

Since this book focuses on the historical development of the Chicago Metropolitan Assurance Company, it could not have been completed without the assistance of current and former personnel. I especially want to thank former president Anderson M. Schweich who allowed me access to both company records and personnel; Jesse L. Moman, the coordinator of a brief company history written in 1977, who freely gave his time and help; Lee Bailey, the company "griot," whose knowledge of Chicago Metropolitan's early history proved indispensable; and Josephine King, the current chief executive officer who provided me with vital information concerning Chicago Metropolitan's recent operations. Other current and former personnel who cordially answered my questions include: Albertha Bankhead, Edna Banks, Cleland Brewer, Baker Cole, Herbert W. Cooley, Velma Dominguez, John E. Fitzpatrick, Camora Fletcher, James D. Grantham, George R. Hall, Dorothy Harper, Bowen M. Heffner, Henry Hervey, James S. Isbell, Todd Jackson, Donnie Jones, Robert F.

Jones, Lynn Langston, Jr., Velma "PiJo" Lewis, Joseph Moody, Rumor L. Oden, Leon Sanders, Alzater Timmons, Edward A. Trammell II, Eric Von Battles, Robert Wilson, and Louise Wood. I also want to acknowledge the support of Robert A. Cole, Jr., president of the Metropolitan Funeral Parlors. Mr. Cole shared with me a scrapbook his father made for him and his sister, Roberta, as well as several other family photographs and keepsakes.

Besides individuals associated with institutions of higher learning, libraries, and the Chicago Metropolitan Assurance Company, several long-time black Chicagoans also made an important contribution to this book. These persons shared with me their recollections of what Chicago Metropolitan and other black-owned businesses meant to the African American community. Through the gracious assistance of Robyn Martin, former social service coordinator of the William Dawson Nursing Home (on Chicago's South Side), I elicited valuable information from the following individuals: Buelah Boyd, Kathryn Boyd, Almetta Dooley, Anna Evans, Curtis Flucker, Vivian Hart, Edwina Helm, Bessie Hoggans, Jack Johnson, Willella Lomax, Nancy Long, Vida Madison, Bertha McMillan, Emma Richmond, John Smith, Fred Spencer, Beatrice Wright, and Jerry Moses Young, Jr. In addition to my Dawson Nursing Home informants, other long-time black Chicagoans who assisted this project were: Dr. Marjorie Stewart Joyner, now deceased, who was a friend and confidante of both Madame C. J. Walker and Dr. Mary McLeod Bethune; Clarence M. Markham, a co-founder of the *Negro Traveler and Conventioneer* magazine in 1943; Etta Moten-Barnett, former show-business notable and widow of Claude A. Barnett, the founder of the Associated Negro Press; and Dolores J. Weems, my mother and life-long Chicago resident.

It goes without saying that I'm grateful to my wife, Clenora, and daughter, Sharifa, for putting up with my "inaccessibility" while I completed this manuscript. Also, I want to thank my parents and sisters for their long-time encouragement. In addition, I have truly appreciated the special support of my friends, colleagues, and in-laws.

Finally, I want to acknowledge the guidance of both Weathers Y. ("Sonny") Sykes and Professor Thomas W. Shick. "Sonny" Sykes, a fellow University of Wisconsin-Madison graduate and former senior vice-president/Operations of Chicago Metropolitan, facilitated my entry into the inner realm of the company. Thomas W. Shick, formerly of the Afro-American Studies Department at the University of Wisconsin-Madison, helped facilitate my development as a historian. Although they will never read this book, I hope it meets their standard of excellence.

INTRODUCTION

The Chicago Metropolitan Assurance Company is one of America's oldest black-owned businesses. This company, founded in 1925 as the Metropolitan Funeral System Association, initially provided economical burial insurance to working-class black Chicagoans. Over time, Chicago Met's base of operations expanded to serve African Americans throughout the state of Illinois and in neighboring Indiana and Missouri.[1] Moreover, the company has evolved from a burial insurance association into a legal reserve insurance company with a diversified coverage portfolio.

Chicago Metropolitan's birth and development paralleled the dramatic growth of black Chicago, or what Horace Cayton and St. Clair Drake called the "Black Metropolis,"[2] during the early to mid-twentieth century. Fueled by a steady stream of southern migrants, Chicago's black population grew from 44,109 to 812,637 between 1910–1960.[3] While many of these newcomers were fleeing southern racism, they were not necessarily fleeing the influence of southern black culture. Consequently, one southern black tradition, securing insurance through membership in a mutual aid or fraternal organization,[4] remained foremost in the minds of individuals seeking to establish themselves in a hostile and impersonal new environment.

Previous studies of individual African American insurance companies have tended to focus upon four distinct aspects of corporate development. First, they have (correctly) stressed that black insurance companies evolved from a historic tradition of mutual aid. Second, they have demonstrated black insurers' genuine attempts to perpetuate economic and social cooperation among African Americans. Third, they have offered a (relatively rare) glimpse at the internal operations of historic African American business enterprises. Finally, previous examinations of black insurance companies have addressed the issue of competition with white companies for prospective black policyholders.[5]

This history of the Chicago Metropolitan Assurance Company will discuss the various programs and projects established by the company (over time) to enhance black community life. Also, readers will be provided with an inside look at the historical development of a major African American enterprise. Yet, because Chicago Metropolitan's historical development (unlike that of previous companies examined) appeared linked to gambling and gambling profits, this unique issue will be addressed. Moreover, the current study places greater emphasis than its predecessors on the competition between black and white insurance companies, especially in the wake of racial integration.

While the founders of the North Carolina Mutual Life Insurance Company, the Supreme Life Insurance Company, and the Atlanta Life Insurance Company appear to have been individuals with impeccable reputations,[6] Chicago Metropolitan's first two presidents are controversial historical figures. Both Daniel M. Jackson and Robert A. Cole, Sr., secured personal fortunes through gambling.[7] Moreover, both men used gambling winnings to buttress the Metropolitan Funeral System Association's financial situation. To some, this might taint the company's historical significance. But an objective examination of twentieth-century black entrepreneurs offers a rationale for, if not condones, the Metropolitan Funeral System Association's unique source of additional working capital.

It is widely acknowledged that African American entrepreneurs have had, and continue to have, difficulty in gaining access to capital for business start-up and expansion. This problem of discriminatory lending practices by white-controlled banks appeared especially acute during the early twentieth century. Consequently, some pioneer black businessmen felt compelled to raise capital through such creative means as gambling. Although gambling, in many instances, results in negative consequences, some black entrepreneurs, such as Dan Jackson and Robert A. Cole, used their expertise in this area to make a positive contribution to their community.* Also, when one observes how various states currently use gambling winnings, commonly referred to as the "lottery," to finance a variety of worthwhile projects, the activities of Jackson and Cole seem far from dishonorable. In fact, it appears that all entrepreneurs, considering the risks involved with business enterprise, are gamblers at heart. (Not to mention all the "respectable" people who "play" the stock market.)

Chicago Metropolitan's early use of gambling winnings, while uncommon, reflected the self-help ideology that permeated the operations of all black insurance companies. Yet despite black insurers' historic focus

---

*An example of how Robert A. Cole and other black gambler/entrepreneurs promoted meaningful community projects was their resuscitation of the Negro Baseball Leagues during the Great Depression (see chapter 4).

on community uplift, they have not operated within a racially insulated vacuum. These companies, even during the height of American apartheid, operated within the framework of American capitalism. Therefore, general market considerations, as well as (internal) self-help ideology, influenced the growth and development of Chicago Metropolitan and other black firms.

It is well documented that the birth of the black insurance industry, while inspired by African Americans' mutual aid tradition, can also be traced to the militant "Anglo-Saxonism" that emerged in late nineteenth-century America. Ironically, before an increasing number of studies began to predict the imminent extinction of African Americans, the embryonic life insurance industry competed with African American mutual aid societies for the business of newly freed blacks. Yet by the turn of the twentieth century, companies such as Prudential and Metropolitan Life, citing the disproportionately high mortality rates of an "unfit race," either abandoned black consumers or charged them higher premiums than whites.[8] Thus, mainstream companies' designation of African Americans as "bad insurance risks" provided a direct impetus for the establishment of commercial, non-fraternal, black-owned companies.

Because black insurance companies provided African Americans with a needed service during the first half of the twentieth century, they emerged as the most successful instance of black economic development.[9] Still, despite their stature among African Americans, black insurance companies, within the realm of American business, operated at a competitive disadvantage. Merah S. Stuart's 1940 classic *An Economic Detour: A History of Insurance in the Lives of American Negroes* illuminated the disadvantageous position black companies operated from during the "Jim Crow" era.

First and foremost, Stuart cited (and criticized) the white racism that relegated black insurance companies to serving only the poorest segment of the American people.[10] Also, Stuart sorrowfully conceded that white insurance companies, benefiting from their aura (and substance) of greater prestige and stability, actually attracted more black customers than the black-owned firms.[11] For example, in 1938 the weekly premium income of the leading twenty-nine black insurance companies was $248,910. Yet Stuart estimated that blacks paid $995,640 in weekly premiums to white companies during the same year.[12] In apparent exasperation, Stuart lamented:

Every one of the $248,910 paid into Negro companies is free to perform its natural function of helping to create employment to which the qualified among the group that spends it are eligible. Every one of the $995,640 paid by Negroes into white companies, as soon as paid over the line, becomes earmarked for discrimination against employment of the group that spends it; and the employment these dollars help to create is forbidden fruit to the sons and daughters of those who each week unthoughtfully pay this price to keep the doors of opportunity closed against their own.[13]

Since black-owned insurance companies never really monopolized the black consumer market, even during enforced racial segregation, the simultaneous mid-twentieth century improvement in African American life expectancy,[14] along with the embryonic Black Freedom Movement, posed ominous implications for black insurers. Robert H. Kinzer and Edward Sagarin's 1950 study, *The Negro in American Business: The Conflict between Separatism and Integration*, offered a cogent analysis of the role of African American insurance companies in a changing society.

While black companies, according to Kinzer and Sagarin, benefited from a decline in African American mortality rates, this demographic improvement could also persuade white-owned companies to ". . . go after the Negro business much more aggressively than they have done in the past."[15] Moreover, in an integrated society, black insurance companies would be no more ". . . than the small business periphery of the larger insurance business."[16]

Robert C. Puth's 1968 study of the Chicago-based Supreme Liberty Life Insurance Company addressed, among other things, the issue of competition between black and white insurance companies. According to Puth, Supreme Life agents, during the company's early years, secured a significant number of policyholders by appealing to the nationalist tendencies of the black masses. Specifically, Puth asserted:

In selling, agents had one very effective approach—the appeal to "Race Pride." They would point out that while other firms might accept applications for insurance, they would not hire Negro agents or employees. Liberty Life, on the other hand, was owned, managed and staffed by Negroes, and its mortgage operations assisted Negroes in their efforts to obtain better housing. The agents could point to the fact that Negroes had white-collar jobs with Liberty Life, including the highest executive positions in the firm. This appeal was widely used by Negro firms, and was quite effective against "outside" competition.[17]

Yet by the 1960s, as overt racial barriers began to fall, Supreme Life and other black companies were forced to develop new strategies to retain black policyholders and, hopefully, attract white consumers. Significantly, Puth concluded his study by expressing doubt as to whether Supreme Life and other black companies could effectively compete in an open insurance marketplace.[18]

Linda P. Fletcher's 1970 study, *The Negro in the Insurance Industry,* cast further doubt on the ability of African American insurance companies to thrive in an integrated society. In fact, Fletcher asserted that black companies faced a double threat from white competitors. She declared:

> White insurers anxious to increase their ratio of Negro employees have found in the Negro companies' personnel a prime source of proficient and experienced black workers. The Negro firms are thus major targets for a vast number of recruiters. Concurrent with the Negro concerns' difficulties in preventing a crippling drain on their work force are increasing efforts by white firms to capture the Negro market. *The combined effect of these two events will ultimately have an impact—and probably detrimental—on those Negro firms that have pioneered in developing both the Negro life insurance market and employment skills and opportunities among black employees.*[19] (Emphasis mine)

Similar to Kinzer and Sagarin, Linda Fletcher, too, has proven to be an accurate forecaster concerning black insurance companies. Since the 1970s, black insurers have suffered a significant decline in stature within the larger industry.[20] Ironically, Walter B. Weare's 1973 study, *Black Business in the New South: A Social History of the North Carolina Mutual Life Insurance Company,* the first major book-length examination of a single black insurance company, appeared when the profitability of black insurance companies began to spiral downward.

Weare's study of North Carolina Mutual focused on company history before the 1950s. Still, *Black Business in the New South* did address the implications of racial integration (and increased white competition) on NCM, the country's largest black insurer.

Noting that the "black entrepreneur looked to integration as the warrior looked to peace,"[21] Weare asserted that North Carolina Mutual responded to the changing racial climate cautiously. On one hand, NCM, optimistic about reaching white consumers, muted its earlier focus on racial solidarity. Yet at the same time, North Carolina Mutual sought to maintain its historic ties with the black community.[22]

Alexa Benson Henderson's 1990 study of the Atlanta Life Insurance Company also discussed the dilemma posed to black insurance companies by racial integration. Atlanta Life, described by Henderson as a "Guardian of Black Economic Dignity," appeared more reluctant than North Carolina Mutual to de-emphasize its "racial mission." Still, by the 1980s, Atlanta Life's survival appeared based upon more than appealing to black consumers. Professor Henderson noted:

> In the 1980s, even as the present leaders are concerned with the future, probing new markets and new mergers, they are very mindful of the heritage and obligations of a race enterprise. . . . Despite the dilemma of changing markets and cultural settings . . . Atlanta Life has chosen to maintain faith with its traditions and ethnic identity, to make itself more attractive to the black market and at the same time, to search for viable formulas to help meet the challenges of the 1980s, especially those involving the need to capture a larger share of the total market.[23]

Racial integration also had a significant impact upon the Chicago Metropolitan Assurance Company. Similar to other black companies, Chicago Metropolitan attempted to reach white customers while retaining its black community base. During the 1970s, the company's entry into the group insurance market indicated some progress in this area. Still, by the 1980s working-class blacks remained the company's chief constituency. Moreover, the economic problems experienced by the African American masses during the Reagan and Bush administrations adversely impacted Chicago Met and other black insurers.*

Ironically, while it appears that the future health of black insurance companies is linked with attracting more non–African American clients, economic (racial) integration has been, and probably will continue to be, a one-way affair. While white-owned companies have made considerable inroads among black consumers, whites remain apprehensive about doing business with African American insurance companies.[24] Consequently today's black insurance companies find themselves caught in a de facto, if not de jure, version of the "economic detour" described by M. S. Stuart more than fifty years ago.

As Chicago Metropolitan and other African American insurance companies prepare to enter the twenty-first century, their future appears uncertain. Increased competition from white companies (for black poli-

---

*See the Epilogue for a discussion of this phenomenon.

cyholders), has had a truly negative effect upon black firms. Some black insurance industry insiders speculate that before the year 2000, the majority of existing African American companies will vanish either through merger or liquidation.[25] In fact, as chapter 7 indicates, between 1985 and 1992, six major black insurers (including Chicago Metropolitan) merged with stronger black or white companies. Moreover, the top three black insurance companies, North Carolina Mutual, Atlanta Life, and Golden State Mutual of Los Angeles, have experienced a significant recent decline relative to the larger insurance industry. While it would be tragic if African American insurance companies were to disappear, it would be more tragic if they were to disappear without their vital historical role being fully documented. The following examination of the Chicago Metropolitan Assurance Company has been written with this in mind.

BLACK BUSINESS
IN THE BLACK METROPOLIS

I

THE METROPOLITAN FUNERAL SYSTEM ASSOCIATION, 1925–1946

The Metropolitan Funeral System Association between the years 1925 and 1946 provided economical burial insurance to thousands of working-class black Chicagoans. Although its founders were not formally trained insurance professionals, they were entrepreneurs who correctly perceived a need for the company's service. Moreover, the leadership of the Metropolitan Funeral System Association used innate business acumen to address a variety of internal and external threats to the company's survival. By the mid-1940s, despite the company's early association with gambling, MFSA stood as a respectable, growing, African American enterprise.

The Metropolitan Funeral System Association represented one of many similar companies in Chicago (some of whom predated the MFSA). The proliferation of black-owned insurance companies in this city were a direct consequence of the World War I "Great Migration." As Chicago's African American population exploded, black insurance professionals, who had previously worked for local white-owned companies, developed black-owned firms to cater to an expanding consumer market. The first black Chicago insurance companies were the Underwriters Mutual Life Insurance Company, established in November 1918; the Pyramid Mutual Life Insurance Company, founded in February 1919; and the Liberty Life Insurance Company, which commenced business during the summer of 1919.[1]

While massive southern black migration to Chicago excited the aspirations of local African American entrepreneurs, it often had a less salutary effect upon the migrants themselves. These newcomers, because of Chicago's system of residential racial segregation, were forced to reside in the South Side "Black Belt."[2] As more black migrants streamed into Chicago, the "Black Belt" grew in population, but not in geographic space. Since many of the buildings in the black community were already dilapidated and filthy, severe overcrowding contributed to widespread disease and death.

By the mid-1920s, the negative health effects of the "Great Migration" in Chicago had become a municipal embarrassment. In June 1926, Dr. Herman Bundeson, Chicago's health commissioner, issued a bulletin which revealed that black Chicagoans' death rate (22.5 per 1,000) closely resembled Bombay, India's (25.4 per 1,000). Significantly, these figures stood in marked contrast to a citywide death rate of 11.5 per 1,000.[3]

Chicago's first black insurance companies helped to ease the financial costs associated with this appalling demographic situation. Still, their assistance appears to have been limited. Because of financial constraints, these companies tended to cater to specific socio-economic groups. For instance, Liberty Life, the most prestigious black Chicago insurance company during this period, focused on serving the black middle class.[4] Unfortunately, the (largely uninsured) working poor, not the middle class, were unduly represented in black Chicago death statistics. This disturbing state of affairs led to the birth and development of the Metropolitan Funeral System Association (MFSA).

The co-founders of the Metropolitan Funeral System Association, Otto Stevenson and Daniel Jackson, were men from divergent backgrounds. Stevenson was an obscure local entrepreneur whose background remains largely unknown.[5] Dan Jackson, on the other hand, was one of Bronzeville's* most prominent and notorious figures. Besides owning a successful funeral home, Jackson, by the 1920s, was the acknowledged czar of black Chicago gambling activities and a close friend and political crony of three-time Republican Mayor William Hale "Big Bill" Thompson.[6]

Despite their differences, Otto Stevenson, in 1925, convinced Daniel Jackson to help him establish a burial insurance association. This business, a derivative of mutual aid and beneficial societies, enabled persons with limited incomes to have a decent funeral.[7] Jackson agreed to provide funerals for deceased policyholders and Stevenson assumed responsibility for selling burial insurance policies.

On the surface, it appeared unusual that Daniel Jackson, one of black Chicago's premier businessmen, would enter into such an arrangement

---

*This was south-side "black" Chicago's nickname during this period.

with the apparently upstart Otto Stevenson. However, there were two factors which seem to have induced Jackson's cooperation with Stevenson.

First, Dan Jackson, by 1925, appeared increasingly frustrated about a downturn in his gambling interests. For years his close friend "Big Bill" Thompson had protected Jackson from police harassment. However, when Democrat William Dever upset Thompson in the 1923 mayoral election, both Thompson and Jackson suffered. Dever, who ran on a reform platform, made closing down black Chicago gambling operations a top priority.[8] Jackson's resulting loss of income subsequently led him to seek a "legitimate" means to replace declining gambling revenues.

Besides financial considerations, Jackson agreed to work with Otto Stevenson because the proposed burial insurance association would provide a needed service to low-income black Chicagoans. Dan Jackson, despite his shady reputation as a gambling kingpin, had also gained notoriety for his personal benevolence. He regularly donated money, food, and other provisions to Bronzeville's less fortunate.[9] Consequently, his decision to work with Stevenson seemingly melded Jackson's interests in making money and helping black Chicago's working poor.

The Metropolitan Funeral System Association quickly became popular among black Chicagoans. MFSA, for a minimal $0.15 weekly premium, offered individuals a future burial by Dan Jackson.[10] In addition, the company provided prospective policyholders the option of a southern burial.[11]

Although the fledgling Metropolitan Funeral System Association attracted a considerable number of policyholders, the company's early success proved illusory. Otto Stevenson, apparently unaware of actuarial tables and driven by a desire to quickly expand MFSA's influence and stature, accepted any and all burial insurance applicants. Unfortunately, many of the company's early policyholders were sick individuals who died shortly after buying their burial policies. The premiums they paid did not come close to covering a funeral's actual cost. Also, all policyholders, regardless of age, paid the same $0.15 weekly premium.[12] Thus, the Metropolitan Funeral System Association, within a year of its founding, fell into dire financial straits.

Otto Stevenson, a man of limited means, could not use personal funds to counteract MFSA's growing problems. Thus, he abandoned his financially troubled brainchild and returned to obscurity. However, Jackson, rather than allow the company to fall by the wayside, decided to personally maintain the Metropolitan Funeral System Association. His belief that the company provided a needed service to working-class black Chicagoans, along with the rejuvenation of his gambling clubs after "Big Bill" Thompson's successful 1927 mayoral reelection campaign, prompted Jackson to take this questionable financial step.[13]

Although Dan Jackson had committed himself to resuscitate the ailing MFSA, the re-invigoration of his South Side gambling interests allowed him less time to scrutinize the Metropolitan Funeral System Association's affairs. Still, Jackson's desire to see the company survive motivated him to seek someone to manage MFSA full-time. During the summer of 1927, Jackson asked Robert A. Cole, the manager of his most prosperous gambling club, to oversee the fledgling MFSA.[14]

Robert Alexander Cole, destined to become one of Chicago's most influential black businessmen, had an unusual rise to prominence. Born on October 8, 1882, in Mount Carmel, Tennessee, Cole attained only a fourth grade education. He spent most of his childhood helping his parents, Robert and Narcissa Cole, eke out a tenuous existence as sharecroppers. Despite young Cole's limited educational background, he wanted a future other than farming. When Cole reached the age of seventeen, armed with a desire to "be somebody," he left home to seek his fortune.[15]

The first stop on Cole's rise to prominence was Paducah, Kentucky, where he found employment in a machine shop. Within a year he had been promoted to foreman. Yet it became apparent that under the South's racial code his opportunities there were limited. A bit disconcerted, but all the wiser, he left Paducah and spent the next few years as a roustabout. It appears likely that Cole developed his legendary fondness for gambling during this period of his life.

In 1905, Cole arrived in Chicago seeking the wider opportunities the city reputedly offered blacks. After working briefly as a busboy, Cole secured employment as a Pullman porter. Cole later claimed that his twenty years with Pullman compensated for his lack of formal education because he could talk to business executives and observe their actions. He ultimately earned a promotion to porter-in-charge, reportedly the highest position an African American male could then attain in the railroad industry. Still, the ambitious Cole left Pullman during the 1920s rather than accept his enhanced, but dead-end, occupational status.[16]

During his service at the Pullman Company, Cole had become acquainted with Dan Jackson, who later hired him to manage the gambling club at 35th and State streets. After observing Cole's managerial talents,

Jackson selected him to manage his Metropolitan Funeral System Association.

Shortly after starting his new job, Cole decided upon a daring course of action. He boldly told Jackson in late 1927 that he wanted to own, rather than simply manage, MFSA. Jackson, preoccupied with his resurgent gambling interests, allowed Cole to purchase the company for $500. The two men agreed, however, that Jackson would continue to provide funerals for the company.[17]

Although Cole's purchase of MFSA demonstrated his solid, if not audacious, belief in himself, he remained aware of his limitations. He knew nothing about the funeral business or selling insurance. Therefore, he asked Fred W. Lewing and Ahmad A. Rayner, both Jackson employees, to join him on the Metropolitan Funeral System Association Board of Directors. Both Lewing and Rayner provided vital expertise. Lewing, a long-time black Chicago entrepreneur, had distinguished himself as MFSA's top agent. Hence, Cole wanted him to train and supervise his company's agents. Rayner, a licensed mortician, provided knowledge about the burial process.[18]

The three men quickly reorganized company operations. At their first Board of Directors meeting, on December 19, 1927, a number of important changes were made. First, Cole, Lewing, and Rayner were officially designated president, secretary, and vice-president/treasurer, respectively. After this perfunctory exercise, the trio then discussed and acted upon new company by-laws compiled by Fred W. Lewing.

Perhaps the most significant change suggested by Lewing involved the company's premium payment schedule. Article III, section 2 of the proposed by-laws called for an age-based differential weekly premium payment schedule (see table 1–1). Lewing believed, and other board members concurred, that such a move would help avoid the catastrophe that resulted from Otto Stevenson's universal fifteen-cent premium. Moreover, article III, section 4 of Lewing's proposal, which the board also approved, stated that future applicants for burial insurance had to complete and sign a detailed medical questionnaire.[19]

Despite an obvious attempt to distance the "new" MFSA from the "old" MFSA, Lewing's proposed by-laws did retain one element of the Stevenson/Jackson administration, the southern burial option. Article I, section 5 stated that policyholders in good standing had the option of being buried within a 1,000 mile radius of Chicago. This stipulation, until it became illegal during the early 1930s, represented a powerful market-

TABLE 1–1
Weekly Premium Schedule,
Metropolitan Funeral System Association,
December 19, 1927

Ages	Premium
2–10	$0.10
11–20	0.15
21–30	0.20
31–40	0.25
41–50	0.30
51–55	0.35
56–60	0.50

Source: *Minutes, Organizational Meeting, Metropolitan Funeral System Association, December 19, 1927.*

ing tool for both the "old" and "new" Metropolitan Funeral System Association. Numerous black Chicagoans, many of whom were recent southern migrants, became MFSA policyholders specifically for this benefit.[20]

After MFSA's new leadership paved the way for improved company operations, additional skilled personnel were needed to implement these plans. Although the re-organized company had a cadre of employees retained from the Stevenson/Jackson administration, the Robert A. Cole–led Metropolitan Funeral System Association immediately sought additional persons willing to take a chance with the fledgling company. The overt discrimination practiced against blacks in the early twentieth-century workplace made the search easier. In Chicago, and other cities throughout the United States, a "job ceiling" relegated blacks to menial positions in mainstream stores, factories, and offices. Consequently, MFSA attracted blacks disinclined to allow arbitrary occupational barriers to stifle their ambition.[21]

The new staff had to sell policies to individuals who could meet the more stringent criteria for burial insurance coverage. Rev. Mansfield Edward Peck, appointed MFSA social service director in 1928, helped make that task easier. Rev. Peck, also affiliated with the Greater Bethel A.M.E. Church, made a point of visiting the relatives of deceased policyholders immediately after the death, again at the funeral, and at least once after the funeral. His ongoing efforts to console and assist the relatives of deceased policyholders apparently achieved widespread notoriety and proved a real asset in attracting prospective clients.[22]

Along with Peck's compassion and Cole's leadership, MFSA succeeded in recruiting new policyholders because it catered to a market desperate for its product. Ridding itself of the negative aspects of the Stevenson/Jackson administration, the company wisely retained its initial mission of serving the black working poor. Moreover, despite the establishment of an age-based premium structure, working-class clients continued to regard MFSA coverage as affordable.[23]

An examination of the company's burial records for the period of August 26, 1926 to December 11, 1928, illustrates MFSA's overwhelming working-class constituency. Of the 165 deceased males buried, only 15, or 9.1 percent, held positions that could be considered professional, skilled, or proprietary in nature. Significantly, 46, or 29.9 percent, of the males buried, were designated as "laborer." Only 3 of the 129 females buried, or 2.3 percent, held positions that were professional, skilled, or proprietary in nature.[24]

Besides the company's re-affirmation to cater to Chicago's sizable black working class, the reorganized MFSA gained popularity because of its commitment to settle claims promptly and fairly.[25] Robert A. Cole, throughout his tenure as president, believed prompt claim settlements resulted in community trust. Thus, even in instances where there appeared to be fraud (persons who misrepresented their age or physical condition on policyholder applications), the company quickly paid the claim.[26] While such a policy appeared risky from a business standpoint, MFSA gambled that "deadbeats" represented a small minority of the community. This wager paid off. Within a relatively short period, the company's claim payment policy contributed to a dramatic increase in the number of policyholders.[27]

MFSA's growing reputation as a solid operation also attracted additional skilled persons seeking a career in insurance. One such person was Lee L. Bailey, a graduate of Alcorn A&M College, who joined MFSA as an agent in December 1928. Bailey, destined to spend nearly forty years with the company, sought employment with the Metropolitan Funeral System Association because of the way they handled his uncle's funeral. Bailey's uncle died only two weeks after being issued a policy. Still, he received a full burial without question. Impressed with the service rendered, Bailey immediately sought and secured employment with MFSA.[28]

By 1929, the Metropolitan Funeral System Association had established itself as a viable institution. The number of policyholders paying regular premiums had grown to the extent that there were optimistic plans of expanding company operations into neighboring states.[29] The sense of transition that characterized company sentiment in 1929 appears to have been partially motivated by Dan Jackson's death on May 17. Since 1925, MFSA's headquarters were located in the basement of Dan Jackson's funeral home at 3400 S. Michigan Avenue. More important, Jackson had given the company credibility by providing burials to deceased policy-holders. Still, Jackson's passing gave MFSA an opportunity to assert itself as a truly independent enterprise.

Immediately after Jackson's death, MFSA took steps to establish its autonomy. In June 1929, Robert A. Cole and Fred W. Lewing began the search for a new company headquarters.[30] Later in the year, MFSA policyholders authorized the company's executive team to seek a means whereby the firm could provide its own funerals, rather than rely on an outside undertaker.[31]

By late 1930, MFSA succeeded in making the transition from its earlier dependency on Dan Jackson. Facilities at 418 E. 47th Street were leased to house MFSA and the Metropolitan Funeral Parlors.[32] Robert A. Cole established this latter company to provide funerals for deceased MFSA policyholders.

The company's move to 47th Street, besides providing additional office space, gave MFSA additional visibility. By 1930, 47th Street began to replace the 35th and State Street district as the center of black Chicago's commercial activity.[33] Yet just when the reorganized MFSA appeared poised to attain new heights of achievement, serious threats to the company's survival surfaced.

On February 28, 1930, Charles Jackson, the brother of the deceased Dan Jackson, filed a suit against the Metropolitan Funeral System Asso-ciation. Charles Jackson, who owned a funeral home at 3800 S. Michigan Avenue, contended that his brother had left his funeral home to him (Charles); consequently, MFSA had no legal right to use Dan Jackson's undertaking equipment. Evidently, MFSA had continued to use the undertaking facilities at 3400 S. Michigan Avenue after Dan Jackson's death.[34]

MFSA responded to Charles Jackson's suit by asserting that Dan Jackson gave them the undertaking equipment before he died. To represent its legal interests in court, MFSA employed the prominent black Chicago law firm of Morris, Dickerson, and Cashin.[35]

Although Charles Jackson's suit contested MFSA's continued use of his deceased brother's undertaking equipment, it appears the equipment dispute was not the real issue at hand. MFSA's early success posed a tremendous economic threat to independent black undertakers (such as Charles Jackson). As the number of MFSA policyholders grew, there was a corresponding decrease in the number of potential clients for undertakers other than Dan Jackson. When Dan Jackson died and MFSA began making arrangements to supply its own funerals, Charles Jackson became especially disturbed. It appears plausible that Charles, as Dan Jackson's brother, may have believed MFSA should have contracted him to supply company funerals.

Besides Charles Jackson's protestation concerning MFSA's use of his brother's equipment, during the subsequent trial he expanded his charges to contest Robert A. Cole's ownership of the Metropolitan Funeral System Association. Jackson claimed Cole never purchased the company from his brother. Moreover, he contended that, as Dan Jackson's legal heir, MFSA belonged to him. Despite these charges, Robert A. Cole successfully proved his legal purchase of the company. Charles Jackson, apparently out of spite, subsequently formed his own Jackson Funeral System Association to compete with MFSA.[36]

Despite Charles Jackson's inability to prove his case against MFSA, his suit did have important implications for Illinois-domiciled burial associations. The Undertakers Association of Chicago, which offered moral support to Charles Jackson during his suit against MFSA,[37] forced the Illinois legislature to pass a 1934 bill that required burial associations to place specific cash surrender values on policies (in lieu of offering strictly burial service) and to give policyholders the option of employing an undertaker other than the one designated by the company.[38] Although this legislation posed a threat to MFSA, the vast majority of company policyholders continued to have their funerals administered by the MFSA-sponsored Metropolitan Funeral Parlors.[39]

While the majority of MFSA employees and policyholders applauded the dismissal of Charles Jackson's lawsuit, there were others who were discontented with the company's leadership. A faction led by Alfred Nelson, an Agency Department superintendent, increasingly believed that Robert A. Cole misappropriated MFSA funds. This unrest led to the establishment of the Metropolitan Policyholders Protective Association (MPPA) in late 1932.[40]

Before he founded the Metropolitan Policyholders Protective Association, Alfred Nelson stood as one of the company's outstanding figures.[41]

Little is known of his background before he joined MFSA during the late 1920s. Still, he rapidly distinguished himself as an agent and by 1930 was an Agency Department superintendent.[42]

Nelson, from his vantage point within the company, became convinced the MFSA board, especially Robert A. Cole, did policyholders a disservice. Nelson believed Cole used policyholders premiums to finance outside interests. He also felt that Cole exploited agents. Nelson could not accept the 1929 provision of salaries for board members,[43] especially since he believed the agents were actually responsible for MFSA's growth. Consequently, Alfred Nelson began a concerted campaign to unseat Robert A. Cole from company leadership.

On December 15, 1932, the Metropolitan Policyholders Protective Association filed a suit for receivership against the Metropolitan Funeral System Association. Among other things, the MPPA suit contended that Robert A. Cole, Fred W. Lewing, and Ahmad A. Rayner illegally diverted funds into outside projects the trio either owned or controlled. MPPA specifically charged that $16,932.51 of MFSA funds were illegally disbursed to the St. Paul, Minnesota, firm of Brown and Bigalow, for printing the *Bronzeman* magazine (see chapter 4), a publication established by Cole, Lewing, and Rayner, and that $61,660.14 had been paid to the Robert A. Cole–owned Metropolitan Funeral Parlors for funerals provided by MFSA.[44] This second charge implicitly decried the profits Cole received as owner of the undertaking establishment that supplied company funerals.

The Metropolitan Policyholders Protective Association's suit against MFSA, while based upon specific allegations, reflected wider community criticism of Robert A. Cole. Because of his lack of formal education, Cole elicited the ridicule of some black Chicagoans. Since genteel behavior has historically been expected of black professionals and businessmen,[45] Cole's "free spirit" demeanor further aggravated his critics.[46] Still, the greatest indictment of Robert A. Cole by his critics was his fondness for gambling.*

The evidence suggests that the mysterious nature of Cole's gambling activities provided the Metropolitan Policyholders Protective Association with ammunition in its suit against MFSA. Company records reveal that

---

*Although gambling in black Chicago during this period has primarily been associated with "policy," Cole specialized in cards—poker and blackjack.

the reorganized Metropolitan Funeral System Association operated for two years before salaries were provided for Cole, Lewing, and Rayner.[47] The obvious question is, how was the MFSA Board of Directors compensated for its duties from December 1927 to December 1929? It appears plausible that Fred W. Lewing, as first Agency Director, may have received a percentage of agent collections. Lewing also serviced his own debit* (in the evenings) until the mid-1930s. It also appears reasonable to assume Ahmad A. Rayner, while ostensibly MFSA vice-president, remained on Dan Jackson's payroll because of his undertaking expertise. Robert A. Cole's financial status during this period, however, appears nebulous. Did he equate his ownership of MFSA with the right to use company funds for personal use? Or was he such a successful gambler that he lived off his winnings until MFSA provided him a regular salary?

A clue to Cole's major source of income appeared in the November 24, 1931, examination of the Metropolitan Funeral System Association by the Illinois Department of Insurance. This probe, which surveyed company operations from December 1927 to September 30, 1931, noted that among MFSA's liabilities was a note payable to Robert A. Cole for $18,166.62. Cole apparently loaned the company this sum to renovate its new headquarters at 418 E. 47th Street.[48] Considering the salaries provided for Cole, Lewing, and Rayner at the December 29, 1929, general (policyholders) meeting were $250, $100, and $100 per week, respectively, it seems obvious that Cole had a substantial outside income source. Since Cole had no expertise as an agent or undertaker, it appears his outside income came from gambling, an activity he reportedly excelled at. Moreover, because of gambling's relative secrecy, the MPPA's concern over Cole's income seems understandable.

Cole's penchant for gambling also appears related to MPPA's protestation of his apparent profiteering as president of the Metropolitan Funeral Parlors. MFSA, after Dan Jackson's death, decided to provide its own funerals rather than contract with another outside undertaker.[49] According to company legend, Cole, Rayner, and Charles Jackson played poker to determine who would have the controlling interest in the subsequent Metropolitan Funeral Parlors. As the story goes, Cole "won"

---

*A "debit" is the sum of premiums payable within a stipulated time period (usually a week) by policyholders in the agent's geographic area. In industry parlance, the term "debit" is frequently used to describe the geographic area in addition to the premiums to be collected from the area's policyholders.

the Metropolitan Funeral Parlors because of his gambling expertise.[50] This is an entertaining and provocative narrative, which represented one of Bronzeville's hottest rumors during the early 1930s. Yet it appears Cole, in lieu of being repaid the $18,166.62 he loaned MFSA in 1930, requested ownership of the Metropolitan Funeral Parlors. This assertion is borne out by two documents. The first is the June 10, 1932, Illinois Department of Insurance Examination of MFSA that surveyed operations from September 30, 1931, to May 31, 1932. The second document is the corporate charter of the Metropolitan Funeral Parlors filed June 6, 1932.

Although the November 24, 1931, Department of Insurance Examination of MFSA listed a "Note Payable" to Cole for $18,166.62, the June 10, 1932, report revealed no such transaction.[51] Moreover, since MFSA's June 10, 1932, financial statement did not list a payment to Cole for the loan in question, this money apparently "vanished." Yet, the corporate charter of the Metropolitan Funeral Parlors (designated the System Burial Company) listed Robert A. Cole as the principal stockholder of the new company.[52]

Despite a debatable conflict of interest, Cole's subsequent control of the Metropolitan Funeral Parlors appears to have been accomplished through shrewdness, rather than mean-spirited activities. It is also reasonable to assume that even though the Metropolitan Policyholders Protective Association's suit against MFSA possessed theoretical merit, its motivation may have been based as much upon jealousy (of Cole) as upon righteous indignation. Regardless of MPPA's motivation, it failed to substantiate its charges in the subsequent trial.

The Metropolitan Policyholders Protective Association, after losing in the courts, took its case directly to MFSA employees and policyholders. At the January 15, 1934, annual policyholders meeting, MPPA leader Alfred Nelson announced his candidacy for board membership. Despite his vehement denunciation of the Cole administration, those present overwhelmingly rejected Nelson's bid for board membership. When the meeting also tabled Nelson's motion that salaries for board members be abolished, Nelson and his followers suffered further humiliation.[53]

After this crushing defeat, Nelson left MFSA and persuaded the longtime black Chicago undertaking firm of Kersey-McGowan to assist him in establishing a burial association to compete against MFSA.[54] To further his aims, Nelson attempted to "raid" MFSA of its top agents through monetary incentives.[55] Unfortunately, for Alfred Nelson, the Kersey-McGowan Funeral Association experienced an early demise.

Nelson, in a last ditch attempt to "get even" with the MFSA leadership, made a bizarre appearance at the company's January 16, 1939, annual meeting. Declaring "God" directed him to speak out against the board, Nelson denounced MFSA's leaders as liars and thieves. When attorney James B. Cashin, (a member of the legal team that successfully defended the company against suits by Charles Jackson and MPPA) moved to have Nelson ejected from the meeting, Nelson replied, "I . . . dare any sucker to put their hands on me." To avoid a free-for-all, Nelson received a half hour to state his case.[56]

After Nelson delivered a disoriented tirade, during which he asserted the MFSA board had him beaten up because he "knew too much, " James Cashin declared, "We have been troubled with this brother for many years. Sometimes he reminds me of the seven year locust." Nelson, who then had to be restrained from physically attacking Cashin, dared to be ejected from the meeting. Finally, Nelson, in a gesture that offered substantive evidence of his mental instability, stated, "If you don't like it [his behavior], make a motion that I be put out, and I will go out." James B. Cashin immediately made a motion according to Nelson's request, which the meeting promptly seconded and carried. Although Nelson appeared hesitant about leaving, he eventually gathered up his belongings and left, heading toward a troubled obscurity.[57]

Although the Metropolitan Funeral System Association successfully withstood the legal challenges of Charles Jackson and the Metropolitan Policyholders Protective Association, the company faced yet another contemporary threat to its survival. When Wall Street "crashed" on October 29, 1929, its reverberations were felt throughout the world. The ensuing Great Depression had an especially deleterious effect upon Bronzeville. Not only did once prosperous black businessmen lose their fortunes,[58] but countless working-class black Chicagoans lost their jobs.[59] The growing unemployment of Chicago's black workers posed an especially serious threat to MFSA because they represented the company's chief constituency.

Despite this potentially disastrous situation, MFSA, for a variety of reasons, survived the Depression. Moreover, the U.S. insurance industry as a whole fared much better than other commercial enterprises. For example, in 1932 alone there were 32,000 business failures. Yet only 39 insurance companies expired during the entire decade. Conservative investment policies, coupled with conservative, stable, leadership, seemed to explain the insurance industry's relative immunity to this economic disaster.[60]

General Manager/Secretary Fred W. Lewing deserves most of the credit for the company's survival during the tenuous 1930s. Metropolitan Funeral System Association employees regarded Lewing as a stern task-master who would not accept mediocrity, especially from agents.[61] Quick to use profanity to make a point, Lewing would often state afterwards, "If I hurt anybody's feelings, I beg your pardon, but I still mean it."[62]

While Lewing's heavy-handed managerial technique may appear crude by today's standards, his gruff demeanor elicited increased productivity, rather than mutinous behavior, among 1930s MFSA personnel. There were two apparent reasons for Lewing's managerial success. First, Lewing never expected more of company personnel than he expected of him-self. Lewing, despite occasional grumbling among employees concerning his administrative methods, received universal respect for his drive and skill. His earlier exploits as the company's first outstanding agent were common knowledge. Consequently, when Lewing urged agents to cover Bronzeville "like the morning dew" during the Depression, his words were taken seriously.[63]

Lewing's even-handedness represented the second characteristic of his managerial triumph. All MFSA personnel, including Robert A. Cole, felt the sting of Lewing's admonitions. At times, Lewing and Cole's relationship seemed especially tense.[64] Still, Cole and other company personnel realized that behind Lewing's gruff demeanor, stood a man who truly loved the Metropolitan Funeral System Association and wanted to see it survive.

Besides the company's strong leadership, as embodied by Fred Lew-ing's efforts, MFSA survived the Great Depression because of burial insurance's continued viability. Although the 1930s death rate among blacks in Chicago declined slightly from 1920s levels, it remained high compared to white death rates (see table 1–2). Consequently, any com-pany that sought to ease the burden of death in the African American community remained an important entity. The evidence suggests that thousands of hard-pressed Bronzeville residents considered weekly MFSA premiums to be a necessity, rather than a luxury.

The Metropolitan Funeral System Association's flexibility with policy-holders represented another reason it survived the Depression. The company, realizing a sizable portion of its constituency were recently unemployed and on relief, adopted a liberal premium payment policy when appropriate. MFSA agents, in lieu of cash, occasionally accepted such items as butter and government "scrip" for premium payments.[65]

TABLE 1–2
**Black and White Death Rate (Exclusive of
Still Births) per 1,000 in Chicago:
1920, 1930, 1931**

Race	1920	1930	1931
Blacks	19.4	15.4	15.3
Whites	12.4	10.0	10.0
Entire City	12.7	10.4	10.4

Source: Charles E. Hall, Negroes in the United States, 1920–1932 *(Washington, D.C.: United States Bureau of the Census, 1935), p. 452.*

In addition to its able leadership, attractive product, and flexible premium payment program, MFSA endured the Depression because it expanded operations through a liberal agent hiring policy. The company's Depression-era policy to give all aspirant male agents a "chance, " proved beneficial to both successful agent trainees and MFSA. During the 1930s, MFSA agents were paid strictly on commission. They received 15 percent of the weekly premiums of new business generated and 20 percent commission on collections of previously established accounts.[66] For an agent to survive, he had to continually sell new policies and collect the weekly premiums on previously sold policies. The pressures from earning a living from commission earnings prompted many newly hired MFSA agent trainees to quit after a relatively short period. Yet those that survived not only helped themselves but the company.

Although MFSA survived tough challenges in both the courts and the streets, it did not emerge from the Great Depression completely unscathed. In October 1929, the company had a reported 70,000 policyholders. Two years later this figure had dwindled to 35,357, a nearly 50 percent lapse rate. By October 1933, the number of policies in force stood at 29,623.[67] The Metropolitan Funeral System Association's high lapse ratio reflected the experiences of other insurance companies (both black and white) during the early years of the Depression.[68]

Notwithstanding problems associated with the early 1930s, MFSA, beginning in 1935, once again experienced significant growth (see table 1–3). It appears that ameliorative "New Deal" programs, such as the Works Project Administration (WPA), contributed to this situation. Many unemployed black Chicagoans, through the WPA, became wage earners again. Thousands of these individuals apparently used some of

TABLE 1–3
Metropolitan Funeral System Association,
1935–1939

	1935	1936	1937	1938	1939
Net Premium					
Income	$393,725	486,388	475,980	523,890	567,118
Payments to					
Policyholders	$81,578	107,319	122,206	123,490	131,250
Number of					
Policyholders	33,210	40,212	45,950	49,727	51,883
Total Admitted					
Assets	$107,669	161,051	229,577	339,414	472,904
Surplus	$87,079	140,530	205,971	313,482	434,037

Source: Examination of the Metropolitan Funeral System Association, Illinois Department of Insurance, January 22, 1940, p. 21; July 30, 1941, p. 24.

their earnings to re-establish (or establish) ties with the Metropolitan Funeral System Association.

Besides the unusual circumstances faced by MFSA during the 1930s, the company had to address relatively mundane problems associated with normal growth and development. As the number of both policyholders and employees grew, the Metropolitan Funeral System Association had to reorganize its administrative structure. The MFSA executive team's lack of experience in operating a large-scale business complicated this process. Robert A. Cole's previous managerial experience consisted of supervising a small number of people. Fred W. Lewing, who had once owned a barbershop and a livery service, brought a small-businessman's orientation to MFSA. Finally, Ahmad A. Rayner, the third member of the initial management team, was a mortician with limited administrative experience.

The situation appeared further muddled at the January 15, 1934, annual policyholders meeting when Rayner indicated his desire to resign from the MFSA Board of Directors. Rayner, who also managed Robert A. Cole's Metropolitan Funeral Parlors, apparently felt unable to hold both positions. Although the irascible Alfred Nelson immediately offered his name in consideration for the vacancy, Rayner nominated Thomas P. Harris, a junior member at the law firm of Morris, Dickerson, and Cashin, to replace him. Harris's subsequent election to the MFSA Board of

Directors represented an important transition in both the company's history and Thomas P. Harris's career.[69]

Thomas Porter Harris, born December 16, 1898, in Columbus, Mississippi, had early aspirations of entering medicine. Yet by the time he graduated from Fisk University (Nashville, Tennessee) in 1922, his primary interest had shifted to business. Moreover, during a subsequent brief stint with a small Arkansas-based insurance company, Harris concluded that a prospective businessman needed legal expertise. Consequently, he applied and gained admittance to the University of Chicago Law School.[70]

After graduating in 1929, Harris secured employment with the law firm of Morris, Dickerson, and Cashin. Although initially he was little more than a clerk for this prestigious black firm, Harris's serious nature and dedication attracted Robert A. Cole's attention during Cole's frequent visits for legal counsel. On Cole's recommendation, MFSA appointed Harris its legal advisor in 1932. While Morris, Dickerson, and Cashin represented the company in court, Harris served as an on-site consultant.[71] Harris's 1934 election to the MFSA board indicated that he distinguished himself in this position. Harris received another vote of confidence at the Board of Directors meeting held immediately following the January 15, 1934, general meeting. The board designated Harris vice-president and general counsel, thus giving him a huge promotion.[72]

Attorney Thomas P. Harris's ascendancy to the MFSA Board of Directors offered still another possible explanation for the company's ultimate survival. Despite the deficiencies of the company's leadership, the MFSA board, as personified by Robert A. Cole, astutely realized its limitations and sought to correct the situation. Although Thomas P. Harris did not have managerial experience within a large company,* he did possess legal expertise. In the wake of MFSA's early legal battles, Cole concluded that the company needed on-going legal expertise to both react to and prevent adverse situations. Besides a major battle with the giant Metropolitan Life Insurance Company of New York during the early 1950s (see chapter 2), Thomas P. Harris's more than forty-year tenure as a board member witnessed a relative dearth of court cases involving the company.

---

*During this period in African American history, it was difficult to find black individuals with expertise in overseeing large business ventures because, quite frankly, there were relatively few large-scale black enterprises. Also, white-owned firms employed few, if any, black managerial staff.

Despite the predominance of males in administrative positions, the efforts of female personnel were equally significant during MFSA's early years. Although women were conspicuously absent from the company's agency force,* they served admirably in a variety of other capacities within the Metropolitan Funeral System Association.

The majority of female employees worked in the Clerical Department. Bronzeville women, between World Wars I and II, had few employment options besides personal service positions or unskilled factory labor.[73] The Metropolitan Funeral System Association and other black companies offered black women an opportunity to earn a living by typing, filing, and bookkeeping, rather than mopping, dusting, and washing.

Members of the company's early clerical force who deserve special mention were Edith Lautier, the Clerical Department's first supervisor; Ada Jones Bowen, MFSA's bookkeeper; Emma Hodge, the clerical worker who processed agents' weekly accounts; Jessye Newman, Thomas P. Harris's personal secretary and recording secretary at official company meetings; and Rosalee Wood, Edith Lautier's successor as Clerical Department supervisor. Mrs. Wood's stature within the MFSA appeared especially significant. Rosalee Wood, during the Depression, reportedly loaned the company a portion of her salary to help pay claims.[74]

Besides their predominance in MFSA's Clerical Department, women also played an important role in Rev. M. E. B. Peck's Social Service Department. This department, besides caring for the families of deceased policyholders, sought to assist living policyholders as well. Four registered nurses, Mary Booth, Anna Giddings, H. D. Motley, and Mrs. F. Bisland, were employed to visit the homes of sick policyholders.[75]

Although women were not employed as agents, Hattie Simms, Julia Taylor, and Mrs. A. G. Campbell worked as MFSA's "investigators." These women, in conjunction with the Social Service and Agency Departments, visited the homes of policyholders having trouble making their premium payments. This trio, in many instances, made arrangements with financially strained policyholders which allowed them to maintain coverage.[76] Considering the economic deprivation associated with the Depression, the work of these women appeared especially significant.

Female personnel, besides their auxiliary roles within the Metropolitan Funeral System Association, also sought to participate in the

---

*Women did not become company (insurance) agents until the 1960s (see chapter 6).

company's decision-making process. Edith Lautier, for example, sought board membership at the January 18, 1937, annual policyholders meeting. Although she ultimately lost to Thomas P. Harris, Lautier received a respectable demonstration of support.[77]

The year 1937, besides witnessing Edith Lautier's unsuccessful bid for board membership, marked the tenth anniversary of the reorganized Metropolitan Funeral System Association. To celebrate this important milestone, the company's Board of Directors began making preparations to construct a new company headquarters.[78]

Both staff and policyholders applauded MFSA's 1930 move from Dan Jackson's basement to a more spacious, two-story structure at 418 E. 47th Street. Still, as the decade progressed, positive sentiment for the 47th Street location waned. Unusually high rent caused this discontent.

Before the company actually conducted business at this location, it financed over $18,000 worth of improvements. Despite this sizable expenditure, they signed a ten-year lease that obligated it to pay $750 per month for the first five years and $800 per month for the balance of the lease. In addition the company had to furnish its own water and heat, as well as pay a $5,000 security deposit.[79]

Despite this less than favorable rental situation, the company did have one source of relief. When Robert A. Cole gained control of the Metropolitan Funeral Parlors, he agreed to pay MFSA $250 monthly rent for use of the first floor at 418 E. 47th Street.[80] Yet in 1935, Cole, whose Metropolitan Funeral Parlors stood in the midst of a business slump, asked MFSA to reduce his monthly rent to $150.[81] The board's subsequent approval of Cole's petition, while helpful to him, placed further strain on MFSA.[82]

Besides the high rent at 418 E. 47th Street, MFSA's decision to construct a new company headquarters appeared based upon a desire to graphically demonstrate the firm's progress. Moreover, the Metropolitan Funeral System Association, by planning to own rather than rent its headquarters, sought to contribute to the black community's real wealth (property ownership).

Before the MFSA board's preliminary decision to construct a new home office complex could come to fruition, two important hurdles had to be cleared. First, because this project would require a significant expenditure of funds, MFSA had to convince the Illinois Department of Insurance that building a new headquarters would not adversely affect the company's ability to pay claims. On October 22, 1937, Robert A. Cole sent a letter to Ernest Palmer, director of the Illinois Department of Insurance, outlining MFSA's plans to construct a new home office. This communique asserted that the total project would cost $102,500 ($17,500 for the lot and $85,000 for actual construction costs). Cole also noted that the proposed structure would be a three-story building. The ground floor would house the Metropolitan Funeral Parlors, the second floor would serve as the Metropolitan Funeral System Association's headquarters, and the third floor would accommodate Bronzeville organizations and businesses desiring office space.[83]

Ernest Palmer, in his December 27, 1937, reply, expressed serious reservations about MFSA's proposal. He believed the project's $102,500 cost, which represented approximately 49 percent of the company's admitted assets (as of September 30, 1937), was too large. In addition, Palmer asserted that the proposed three-story structure would primarily benefit the Metropolitan Funeral Parlors and not the Metropolitan Funeral System Association. Consequently, Palmer rejected MFSA's October 22, 1937, proposal.[84]

Undaunted, MFSA continued its quest for a new headquarters. On April 4, 1938, Cole met with Palmer in Springfield. At this session, Cole presented a modified proposal which stipulated: (1) the project's total cost would be $75,000 ($13,000 for the lot and $62,000 for actual construction costs); (2) the structure would consist of two floors—the ground floor would house MFSA's administrative offices and the second floor would be used as private offices or small apartments; and (3) if the Illinois Department of Insurance accepted this proposal, 45 percent of MFSA's premium income would be placed in a Benefit Account and the company would operate on 55 percent of its income. Cole also assured Palmer that the new home office's cost would be deducted from the 55 percent of premium income designated as operating expenses.[85] On April 8, 1938, Palmer accepted MFSA's modified proposal, noting that the company should begin erection of its new headquarters on or about September 1, 1939.[86]

Once Cole and the Metropolitan Funeral System Association received permission to construct a home office, he next had to secure land upon which to build it. Finding a suitable site appeared especially crucial because the location of a business enterprise largely determined its success or failure. By the late 1930s, the 47th Street commercial strip (from State Street to Cottage Grove Avenue) became Bronzeville's main business thoroughfare. While blacks comprised the vast majority of

shoppers in this area, white merchants, primarily Jewish, virtually monopolized 47th Street commercial outlets.[87] Moreover, as black Chicagoans increasingly patronized 47th Street merchants, the value of 47th
Street commercial property increased. Consequently, most black-owned
enterprises could not afford to purchase a 47th Street location. Moreover, black-owned companies able to rent 47th Street commercial property, such as MFSA, did so at enormous expense. Considering that the
Illinois Department of Insurance had directed the Metropolitan Funeral
System Association to spend no more than $13,000 for the site of its new
headquarters, the company faced the prospect of being relegated to a
peripheral commercial site.

Luckily for MFSA, when it began its search for a new location, Annie
Malone, a noted black Chicago entrepreneur, sought to sell some of her
real estate holdings. Mrs. Malone, who made her fortune by establishing
the PORO Beauty Culture System, experienced financial difficulties
related to the Depression. Consequently Malone, who owned the entire
east side of the 4400 block of South Parkway (now Dr. Martin Luther
King, Jr. Drive) wanted to sell a portion of this holding to relieve her
financial situation.[88] After negotiations with the MFSA board, Malone
sold the southern section of her 4400 South Parkway property for
$12,500.[89]

On August 16, 1939, MFSA formally informed the Illinois Department
of Insurance of its progress toward erecting a new home office. This
communique disclosed two significant revelations. First, since the
company's April 1938 proposal, MFSA's admitted assets had grown from
$250,000 to $413,000. Consequently, the company felt it expedient to
construct a more elaborate structure than it had originally envisioned.
MFSA also informed the department that it intended to build a hall,
rather than apartments, on the proposed edifice's second floor. The
company asserted that the estimated rental income from a hall would
exceed that of apartments. Moreover, if the company's future expansion
warranted larger quarters, the second floor hall could be converted into
offices more easily than apartments.[90]

The Illinois Department of Insurance did not question MFSA's August
16, 1939, status report. Consequently, the MFSA board, at its October 9,
1939, meeting, officially stated its intent to construct new company
headquarters at 4455 South Parkway.[91] The Metropolitan Funeral System
Association stood poised to erect Bronzeville's latest demonstration of
black business success.

During the months immediately following October 1939, black Chicagoans actively monitored the progress of MFSA's undertaking. The Chicago *Defender* utilized photo captions to keep its readers informed of the construction crew's activities.[92] As the winter of 1940 turned to spring, the *Defender*'s portrayal of this project likewise warmed from a matter-of-fact depiction to one of undisguised excitement. For example, the January 6, 1940, *Defender* featured 4455 South Parkway with a photo caption entitled "Metropolitan Funeral System's New Home."[93] Yet, the March 2, 1940, *Defender* chronicled MFSA's project with a photo caption entitled "A New Show Place of the South Side."[94]

Along with the construction of the Metropolitan Funeral System Association's new headquarters at 4455 South Parkway, black Chicagoans witnessed the simultaneous construction of a new Metropolitan Funeral Parlors next door at 4445 South Parkway. The Illinois Department of Insurance had earlier refused to allow the funeral parlors to be a part of the new MFSA headquarters.[95] Consequently, Cole apparently used gambling winnings to finance construction of the new Metropolitan Funeral Parlors.[96] Moreover, in June 1940, the Metropolitan Funeral Parlors, evidently through Cole's winnings, purchased a fleet of new Packard funeral limousines.[97]

The Metropolitan Funeral System Association's new headquarters formally opened on September 7, 1940. A week-long open house, where thousands of black Chicagoans got the opportunity to observe first-hand Bronzeville's newest "showplace, " highlighted this important event. By all accounts, no one expressed disappointment.[98] MFSA's new home, from an architectural standpoint, was state-of-the-art. This building, constructed of white brick, mortar, and tile, was completely fireproof and air-conditioned throughout.[99] Moreover, the first floor, which housed the company's administrative offices, featured the most up-to-date equipment and furnishings, including piped-in music.[100]

Although MFSA's stylish administrative offices duly impressed open house visitors, the elegance of the Parkway Ballroom, located on the second floor, literally stunned black Chicagoans. To reach the ballroom required climbing a winding staircase surrounded by decorative marble walls. The September 7, 1940, Chicago *Defender* offered a description of what awaited visitors to this facility:

> The Parkway Ballroom is easily one of the finest ever built. Its air-conditioned walls are tastefully painted; its comfortable red leather chairs, and the entire scheme for seating make the place a literal palace.

In the rear of the ballroom is a large bar well equipped to care for any number of guests and here the tables and chairs match the color scheme of red plush furniture.[101]

To manage the Parkway Ballroom, MFSA established a subsidiary known as the Parkway Amusement Corporation.[102] The Parkway Ballroom, constructed to provide black Chicagoans with a recreational facility equal to downtown (white) establishments, soon became the hub of Bronzeville social activities (see chapter 4).

Besides the hoopla surrounding the opening of MFSA's new home office, the year 1940 marked the beginning of an extremely prosperous period for the company. Although several agency personnel were subsequently called to duty during World War II, the company experienced dramatic growth between 1940 and 1945. As table 1–4 demonstrates, MFSA's net premium income and number of policyholders more than doubled between 1940 and 1945. The company's total admitted assets and surplus nearly tripled during the same period. It appears plausible to assume that the celebration surrounding the company's new headquarters directly contributed to this growth. Bronzeville residents, who apparently regarded MFSA's new home office as an outstanding racial achievement, evidently became more amenable to company agents who sought their business.

In addition to construction of a new headquarters, two additional circumstances enhanced the Metropolitan Funeral System Association's stature during World War II. First, the company's mortgage loan pro-

TABLE 1–4
Metropolitan Funeral System Association,
1940–1945

	Net Premium *Income*	Payments to *Policyholders*	Number of *Policyholders*	*Surplus*
1940	$623,744	$144,525	56,317	$538,895
1941	696,942	148,815	65,389	640,600
1942	815,032	178,200	74,844	839,046
1943	967,805	192,596	91,074	1,081,182
1944	1,158,099	204,760	109,184	1,380,979
1945	1,328,961	237,757	124,289	1,747,790

Source: Illinois Department of Insurance Examinations of the Metropolitan Funeral System Association, July 30, 1941, p. 24; October 1, 1943, p. 20; September 11, 1944, p. 20; June 24, 1947, p. 11. Minutes, MFSA Annual Meetings, January 15, 1945; January 21, 1946.

gram accelerated between 1940 and 1945. Established in 1938 with a $6,000 loan to Chicago *Defender* editor Robert S. Abbott,[103] by 1945 MFSA had made loans on black Chicago property worth $281,469.19.[104] Since black Chicagoans were then generally unable to secure mortgage loans from white-controlled banks, Bronzeville residents applauded MFSA's growing commitment to make such funds available.

Along with its growing mortgage loan program, the Metropolitan Funeral System Association participated in another popular endeavor during World War II. Between 1942 and 1945, MFSA purchased $1,021,000 worth of United States War Bonds.[105] Moreover, the company's 175 employees averaged 10.3 percent of their salaries in bond purchases. This figure represented a higher employee bond purchase ratio than many corporations holding war contracts.[106]

MFSA's conscientious support of the war effort early on attracted the attention of the U.S. Treasury Department's War Savings Section. The U.S. government subsequently asked Robert A. Cole, who spearheaded MFSA's bond purchase program, to publicly promote the War Bond drive to both black and white audiences. In 1942, Cole spoke to a gathering of over 6,000 employers in Chicago. During this address, Cole forcefully urged greater business support of the war effort.[107]

The Metropolitan Funeral System Association, besides its noteworthy participation in the War Bond drive, made a historic contribution to the U.S. Army's Women's Army Corps (WAC) recruiting effort. In early 1944, MFSA donated $400 for the development of a recruiting poster with the likeness of a black woman. The poster, displayed at 42nd and South Parkway, reportedly represented the first such poster used in the United States.[108]

Significantly, Robert A. Cole's active promotion of the war effort may have been based upon more than patriotism. His efforts in this regard marked the beginning of a conscious attempt to downplay how gambling had contributed to his business success. Moreover, local black media assisted Cole's quest to rehabilitate his image. For example, the December 12, 1942, Chicago *Defender* featured a profile of Cole entitled "From Cabin to Riches"—which failed to mention gambling's centrality in Cole's background.[109]

Despite a dramatic increase in Robert A. Cole's and MFSA's prestige, the World War II era also represented a sad period for the company. By the early 1940s, the hard-driving Fred W. Lewing began to show the ill effects of his exhausting lifestyle. At the July 6, 1943, Board of Directors meeting, the board granted Lewing an extended leave of absence to regain his health. To act in his stead, the board appointed Horace G. Hall to serve as assistant secretary.[110] Hall had been with MFSA since 1925.[111]

Although Lewing returned to work briefly in 1944, his health continued to deteriorate. On April 30, 1945, the MFSA board passed a resolution (with Lewing in mind) which stipulated a Board of Directors vacancy could be filled by the unanimous vote of the remaining directors.[112] On May 22, 1945, Fred W. Lewing died at his home. The next day, Robert A. Cole and Thomas P. Harris selected Horace G. Hall to fill the board vacancy created by Lewing's death.[113]

Fred Lewing's physical decline and death obviously disturbed his friends and associates. Still, he apparently maintained his audacious nature until the end. Lewing demonstrated this when he returned to work briefly in 1944. An overzealous employee had moved into Lewing's office, believing he was not going to recover. Lewing, exhibiting his old fire, upbraided the embarrassed worker, noting, "I'm not dead yet, so get the hell out of my office!"[114]

Lewing's passing, along with the company's expanded operations, represented a transitional period in MFSA's history. The completion of the new home office and the company's dramatic growth between 1940 and 1945 demonstrated that earlier concerns about survival had become outmoded. By late 1945, it seemed clear that MFSA would, indeed, survive. Consequently, the question "how can MFSA better serve the black community?" replaced the earlier question of "will MFSA survive?"

Attorney James B. Cashin delivered the first recorded proposal to expand company operations at MFSA's January 17, 1944, annual meeting. Cashin, after praising President Robert A. Cole, asserted ". . . may we not lose our status of restlessness, restlessness to do, to accomplish things constructive. I have one thing in mind. . . . Let's get a bank."[115]

Although Cashin's bank proposal never got off the ground, exploration for a means to expand company functions continued throughout 1944–1945. These efforts came to fruition at MFSA's January 21, 1946, annual policyholders meeting. Board member Thomas P. Harris, coordinator of the campaign to widen the bounds of company activities, informed the meeting of the board's preliminary decision to issue life insurance policies in addition to burial coverage. Harris asserted that such a move would benefit both MFSA and the larger black community. After subsequent debate, the MFSA board proceeded to make the necessary arrangements to consummate such a maneuver.[116]

On September 30, 1946, the MFSA board, after several months of effort, submitted a copy of the company's amended by-laws to the Illinois Department of Insurance. Among the highlights of this document were:

1. As of October 1, 1946, the company's new name would be the Metropolitan Mutual Assurance Company of Chicago.*

2. In addition to burial insurance, the company would now engage in the business of insurance on the lives of persons and . . . every insurance appertaining thereto or connected therewith and granting, purchasing, or disposing of annuities.

3. The company felt empowered to make such a move because it had grown to the extent that it . . . possessed . . . admitted assets in excess of all liabilities at least equal the original surplus of a Mutual Legal Reserve Life Company.[117]

Besides the above characteristics, the company's reorganization provided additional benefits to members of the old Metropolitan Funeral System Association. Policyholders in good standing were entitled to dividends and additional coverage for loss of eyesight or limbs.[118]

The company's conversion to a legal reserve insurance firm* marked a distinct milestone. The new Metropolitan Mutual Assurance Company of Chicago, in a little more than twenty years, had evolved from Otto Stevenson's fragile undertaking into one of the fastest-growing black enterprises in the United States. Still, the reorganized company sought to enter a line of business in which it had no previous experience. Thus, the challenges it faced in October 1946 were as critical as the challenges associated with its first reorganization in December 1927. Nevertheless, if the company's expansion represented a gamble, President Robert A. Cole relished such a situation.

---

*As a mutual company, policyholders, rather than Robert A. Cole, now owned the assets. Cole did receive compensation for his previous stake in the company. Moreover, he retained the position of president and proprietary owner of the Metropolitan Funeral Parlors.

*As a legal reserve company, the new Metropolitan Mutual Assurance Company of Chicago had to maintain reserves covering policies in force. Thus, the company shifted assets from its "surplus" to a "net reserves" category to satisfy this requirement (Illinois Department of Insurance Examination of the Metropolitan Mutual Assurance Company of Chicago, June 24, 1947, p. 11).

II

THE METROPOLITAN MUTUAL ASSURANCE COMPANY OF CHICAGO, 1947–1952

The reorganized Metropolitan Mutual Assurance Company commenced operations in late 1946 with a spirit of optimism and anticipation. The company, despite its various past problems, stood poised to become an even more important part of Chicago's African American community. Indeed, between 1947 and 1952, the company not only increased its influence in the Chicago area, but extended its services to blacks throughout the state of Illinois. Yet, the Metropolitan Mutual Assurance Company also learned that a growth of corporate stature could also generate a hostile reaction from competitors.

Despite the hopefulness surrounding the Metropolitan Mutual Assurance Company of Chicago's (MMACC) reorganization, a considerable amount of internal uncertainty existed. Since the lack of large-scale managerial experience among the company's leadership represented a major deficiency of the old Metropolitan Funeral System Association, the firm's expansion posed an especially serious challenge. Consequently, the Board of Directors' response to new problems and situations would prove crucial in determining the company's subsequent viability.

Confusion among policyholders was the first major problem created by reorganization. Before October 1, 1946, policyholders paid premiums for a future burial. Despite the Illinois legislature's 1934 ruling, which ostensibly abolished MFSA's control over its members' burials, Robert A. Cole's Metropolitan Funeral Parlors continued to bury the vast majority of deceased MFSA policyholders. There appeared to be two related reasons for MFSA's ability to circumvent Illinois law. First, burial associations were a minor segment of the insurance industry. Consequently, state examiners did not scrutinize their management as closely as that of legal reserve companies. Moreover, since the Metropolitan Funeral

System Association was a black burial insurance association, the state apparently felt even less inclination to thoroughly examine the company's operations. It has been suggested that the Illinois Department of Insurance viewed MFSA and similar black burial associations with condescending amusement.[1]

The reorganized Metropolitan Mutual Assurance Company of Chicago, now under closer scrutiny, had to totally sever all previous ties with the Metropolitan Funeral Parlors. Thus, company policyholders, who had once expected a future burial (by Cole's Metropolitan Funeral Parlors), were now told that their premiums entitled them to a cash benefit of $225 and future dividends. Significantly, some policyholders, critical of the new arrangement, left the company.[2]

Although MMACC had enhanced its insurance capabilities, the company's constituency remained Bronzeville's relatively low-paid working class. Thus, low-cost industrial insurance,* similar in form to previous burial policies, generated the vast majority of Metropolitan Mutual's premium income between 1946 and 1952 (see table 2–1). Still, the MMACC Board of Directors sought to actively promote the company's ordinary or regular life insurance programs. The MMACC board, at their November 25, 1946, meeting, chose Dr. Edward Beasley as the company's medical director. As medical director, the board empowered Beasley to oversee the medical examinations of ordinary insurance applicants.[3] Metropolitan Mutual's hiring of Beasley, a prominent physician who had taught at Northwestern University's Medical School and served as senior pediatrician at Chicago's black-owned Provident Hospital,[4] further enhanced the company's reputation as a solid enterprise.

Besides selecting Dr. Beasley as medical director, Metropolitan Mutual sought to promote its embryonic ordinary insurance program by offering agents lucrative commissions for selling this type of coverage. Compared to the industrial insurance commission of 25 percent of weekly collections and 20 percent of weekly new business (premiums) generated,[5] Metropolitan Mutual agents selling certain ordinary policies were paid

---

*This form of coverage, whose roots are in mid-nineteenth century England, catered to the insurance needs of working class people. Characterized by small, fixed weekly premium payments, industrial insurance provided low-income individuals with limited protection against accidental death and disability. Many industrial insurance policies provided for burial costs. See Malvin E. Davis, *Industrial Insurance in the United States* (New York: McGraw-Hill, 1944).

TABLE 2–1

**The Growth of Industrial and Ordinary Insurance Coverage,
Metropolitan Mutual Assurance Company of Chicago:
1946, 1949, 1951, 1952**

	1946	*1949*	*1951*	*1952*
Industrial Insurance *Written*	$3,232,579	22,757,435	26,740,410	26,055,306
Ordinary Insurance *Written*	$2,600	292,500	843,500	1,414,140
Industrial Insurance *in Force*	$29,358,445	49,092,269	60,182,724	65,177,992
Ordinary Insurance *in Force*	$2,600	925,000	2,007,020	3,015,159

Source: Best's Life Insurance Reports: 50th Annual Edition, 1955–1956 *(New York: Alfred M. Best, 1955), p. 214.*

TABLE 2–2

**Commission Structure for Selling Ordinary Insurance Policies,
Metropolitan Mutual Assurance Company of Chicago,
December 31, 1946**

	RENEWAL COMMISSION			Collection Allowance
Policy Plan	First *Year*	Second *Year*	Third to *Sixth Year*	after First *Year*
Whole Life	45%	6%	3%	2%
Endowment at 65:				
Ages 15–34	45	6	3	2
Ages 35–44	35	5	2	2
20 Payment Life	45	6	3	2
20 Year Endowment	30	4	2	2
Juvenile Endowment at Age 18	25	4	2	2

Source: Illinois Department of Insurance Examination of the MMACC, June 24, 1947, p. 5.

45 percent of the first year's premiums, 6 percent of the second year's paid premiums, and 3 percent of premiums paid during the third to sixth year of the policy (see table 2–2).

Although agents were given a monetary incentive to sell ordinary insurance, this program experienced sluggish growth during the first years of the company's reorganization. Along with the relative poverty of black Chicagoans, agents' lack of sufficient training in selling ordinary insurance represented another reason for this program's moderate beginning. MMACC, before its reorganization, exclusively marketed low-cost burial policies. Some agents, because of previous employment with other companies, had experience in selling ordinary insurance. Still, the majority of MMACC agents had no experience in selling ordinary insurance.

Metropolitan Mutual sought to improve this situation in early 1951 by appointing Leo Blackburn assistant agency director for ordinary insurance. Blackburn, previously employed by the Victory Life Insurance Company (another Chicago-based black insurer),[6] was an ordinary insurance expert. He immediately established classes on the complexities of selling ordinary insurance.[7] These sessions provided Metropolitan Mutual agents with the expertise necessary to market this superior form of insurance coverage.*

Along with employing the services of Leo Blackburn, MMACC solidified its nascent ordinary insurance program by expanding the number of ordinary policies marketed. In 1946, the company offered consumers five types of ordinary insurance policies.[8] By 1952, prospective MMACC policyholders had a choice of eighteen types of ordinary insurance coverage.[9]

In addition to re-coordinating its relationship with policyholders, the reorganized Metropolitan Mutual Assurance Company of Chicago faced the challenge of re-coordinating relationships within the company. The old Metropolitan Funeral System Association was an oligarchy administered solely by its Board of Directors. The Cole/Lewing/Rayner (and later Harris) triumvirate, directly presided over such diverse operations

---

*Compared to industrial insurance, ordinary insurance provided policyholders with significantly higher benefits. For instance, in 1952 the maximum face value of MMACC industrial policies was $900. Yet the maximum face value of ordinary policies was $5,000. It is important to note that ordinary insurance policies were characterized by higher premiums than industrial policies. Also, ordinary insurance, unlike industrial coverage, required a thorough preliminary medical examination.

as the agency force, claim settlements, and mortgage loans. Yet, the company's expansion from a burial association to a legal reserve company prompted a re-evaluation of MMACC's operational structure. Consequently, beginning in 1947, MMACC began to experiment with a departmental administrative structure. This diffusion of administrative power ultimately resulted in greater company efficiency.

The Agency Department immediately benefited from the company's new administrative structure. In 1947, James D. Grantham, a long-time employee who assumed the role of agency director, named Robert F. Jones as special "Field Auditor." Jones, who had been with the company since 1933, became responsible for monitoring agents' paperwork in an attempt to reduce the number of agents with deficits. Jones's duties resulted in the identification and termination of dishonest agents. Moreover, Jones assisted honest agents with deficits in getting their accounts in order.[10]

Dr. Edward W. Beasley's Medical Department offered another instance of efficiency resulting from a departmental administrative structure. Formed in November 1946 to administer physical examinations to applicants for ordinary insurance, in 1947 it became the New Business Department with the additional responsibility of screening applicants for industrial insurance.[11] Although industrial insurance did not require a medical examination, the subsequent closer scrutiny of industrial insurance applicants helped decrease the likelihood of insuring extremely high-risk individuals.

Metropolitan Mutual's Real Estate and Investment Department provided still another instance of enhanced efficiency resulting from the newly established departmental administrative structure. This department, established in 1949 to coordinate both Metropolitan Mutual's burgeoning mortgage loan program and its purchase of securities and bonds, soon became a vital component of company operations.

While President Robert A. Cole took unusual risks as proprietor of the Metropolitan Funeral System Association (see chapter 4), he had to be more restrained as head of a policyholder-owned (mutual) insurance company. Thus, Metropolitan Mutual, similar to other insurance companies (both black and white), developed a rather conservative investment portfolio. As table 2–3 indicates, relatively risk-free bonds represented a significant proportion of company investments from 1950 and 1980.

MMACC's Real Estate and Investment Department, like the company's other newly established departments, featured a skilled individual at its

TABLE 2–3
Investment Data,
Metropolitan Mutual / Chicago Metropolitan,
1950–1980

Investment	PERCENTAGE OF ADMITTED ASSETS						
	1950	1955	1960	1965	1970	1975	1980
Bonds	47	39	52	52	48	50	56
Stocks	1	1	0	1	1	1	2
Mortgages*	37	47	40	40	38	31	22
Real Esate	7	5	3	3	5	3	3

Source: Best's Life Insurance Reports, *1950, pp. 586–87; 1955, p. 214; 1960, p. 354; 1965, p. 262; 1970, p. 273; 1975, p. 312; 1980, p. 378.*

helm. George S. Harris, the Real Estate and Investment Department's first manager, possessed considerable expertise in real estate. A specialist in vacant land acquisition, new construction planning, and mortgage counseling, Harris apparently assisted the company in the construction of its home office. This assumption is supported by Harris's selection as president of the Parkway Amusement Corporation, the MFSA subsidiary that managed the Parkway Ballroom, in 1940.[12]

Regardless of theorizing concerning George S. Harris and the old Metropolitan Funeral System Association, in 1949 he became manager of Metropolitan Mutual's new Real Estate and Investment Department. Harris, a strong proponent of equal housing opportunities for blacks,[13] promoted an accelerated mortgage loan program (see table 2–4). Moreover, he achieved even greater prominence in 1961 upon becoming company president (see chapter 6).

Besides establishing such entities as the New Business and Real Estate and Investment Departments, Metropolitan Mutual, between 1947–1952, increased its number of upper echelon executives from three to five. The Board of Directors, at its September 22, 1947, meeting, designated James D. Grantham as the company's assistant secretary.[14] Grantham, one of the firm's "pioneers," continued to serve as agency director. Later, at its January 15, 1951, meeting, the MMACC board unanimously passed

---

*Because of institutional racism, which all but prohibited African Americans from seeking mortgage money from "mainstream" financial institutions, black insurance companies provided the majority of mortgage money available to prospective African American homeowners during the 1950s and 1960s (and before).

TABLE 2–4
Mortgage Loan Program,
Metropolitan Mutual Assurance Company of Chicago,
1947–1952

Year	Mortgage Investments	Total Loans on Community Property
1947	$254,900	$646,109
1948	722,850	1,252,110
1949	483,100	1,529,049
1950	789,950	2,049,570
1951	787,200	2,478,359
1952	957,100	2,992,752

Source: Minutes, Annual Meetings of the Metropolitan Mutual Assurance Company of Chicago, January 19, 1948; January 17, 1949, January 16, 1950; January 15, 1951; January 21, 1952; January 19, 1953.

resolutions that provided for a future increase in the number of board members and created a new executive position, second vice-president, to he held by Melvin McNairy.[15]

McNairy's rise to prominence appeared especially significant because he spent his entire adult working life with the company. After graduating from high school in 1927, the young McNairy joined the Metropolitan Funeral System Association as an agent. His skill and youthful exuberance enabled him to rise rapidly within the company. Before McNairy's 1951 selection as second vice-president, he served in a variety of positions, including superintendent of agents, supervisor of agent training, and claims manager.[16]

In addition to modifying the company's administrative structure, Metropolitan Mutual's Board of Directors sought to enhance company efficiency by instituting programs designed to improve employee morale. President Robert A. Cole firmly believed that happy workers were more productive workers. Consequently, Metropolitan Mutual employees, during the late 1940s, received benefits that were the envy of other workers throughout Chicago. Among the on-site perquisites made available to all personnel were bowling alleys, a recreation room equipped with pool and billiard tables, a sauna, and a masseur.[17] Since these facilities were available to all personnel, company executives and lower-echelon employees had frequent contact with each other. Because of this regular social interaction among Metropolitan Mutual personnel, much of the traditional distrust that characterized relations between management and labor were absent. Although this situation changed after a strike by company agents in 1957 (see chapters 3 and 5), during the 1940s Metropolitan Mutual personnel considered themselves not only a company, but a "family." (The dynamics of the company "family" will be surveyed in chapter 5.)

The Parkway Ballroom, located on the second floor of the company's home office complex, represented another on-site facility that enhanced employee morale. Despite its regular use by community organizations, Metropolitan Mutual utilized the ballroom for a variety of events, including the annual employees Christmas party, the annual policyholders meeting and informal after-work gatherings.[18]

Notwithstanding the Parkway Ballroom's usefulness and popularity, company executives decided that Metropolitan Mutual should also provide first-class restaurant facilities to its employees and the larger community. Consequently, on October 5, 1948, MMACC sought permission from the Illinois Department of Insurance to build an addition to its home office.[19] On October 13, 1948, N. P. Parkinson, director of the Illinois Department of Insurance, indicated his approval of Metropolitan Mutual's proposal.[20]

At its November 15, 1948, meeting, Metropolitan Mutual's Board of Directors officially authorized the commencement of the restaurant project.[21] This addition to the home office, completed in 1949, bore the name Parkway Dining Room. Known for its courteous waiter service and extensive menu, the Parkway Dining Room further enhanced both employee morale and the company's image in Bronzeville (see chapters 4 and 5).

Besides providing for employees' everyday social needs, Metropolitan Mutual sought to improve company morale (and productivity) by providing for employees' retirement needs. The company's January 15, 1951, annual meeting featured discussion of a proposed pension plan. This proposal, approved by the Board of Directors on January 28, 1952 (to retroactively take effect on January 1, 1952), provided employees, based upon their time spent with the company, with both pension and disability benefits. In addition, this plan established a supplementary annuity program whereby an employee could increase his or her pension through payroll deduction.[22]

Despite a concerted effort to improve the company's administrative structure, insurance offerings, and employee morale, Metropolitan Mutual's expansion outside of the Chicago area, beginning in the early 1950s, represented its most ambitious program. As table 2–5 indicates,

TABLE 2–5
**African American Population
of Selected Illinois Cities,
1940–1960**

	1940	*1950*	*1960*
East St. Louis	16,798	14,304	36,338
Peoria	2,826	3,112	9,584
Springfield	3,357	2,248	5,632

Source: *United States Department of Commerce, Sixteenth Census of the United States: 1940, Volume II*, Population, *pp. 620, 626, 646; Seventeenth Census of the U.S.: 1950, Volume II*, Characteristics of the Population, Part 13, Illinois, *pp. 13–91, 13–93; Eighteenth Census of the U.S.: 1960, Volume I*, Characteristics Of The Population, Part 15, Illinois, *pp. 15–108, 15–112, 15–113.*

the African American population of such smaller Illinois cities as East St. Louis, Peoria, and Springfield increased to the extent that it appeared feasible to seek new clients in these areas. But since Illinois blacks outside of Chicago were generally unaware of the company's reputation, Metropolitan Mutual's cultivation of these "downstate" territories required a special effort.[23]

The company's top agents were enlisted to establish these new territories. When these individuals, also known as "builders," entered an area, they immediately contacted local black ministers requesting permission to speak before their congregations. After briefly describing Metropolitan Mutual's services in these churches, "builders" arranged home visits with individuals desiring additional information.[24]

After Metropolitan Mutual's elite agents made initial contacts and sales in a downstate locale, they were followed by agency personnel designated as the "conservation team." These individuals were responsible for consolidating policies sold by "builders" into an organized debit. Moreover, the "conservation team" had to select and train a local individual to service the newly established debit.[25]

Besides its "builders" and "conservation team," Metropolitan Mutual utilized the services of Moon and Kaemmerle Associates, a New York City public relations firm,* to promote its downstate Illinois

---

*Metropolitan Mutual apparently employed Moon and Kaemmerle because, according to *Scott's Blue Book* (a contemporary black Chicago business and professional directory), there was a dearth of Bronzeville public relations firms during this period. Moreover, it is plausible to assume MMACC employed a New York–based public relations firm to enhance its growing prestige.

expansion program. Events surrounding the 1951 opening of a company branch office in East St. Louis, offered an example of Moon and Kaemmerle's effectiveness.

On January 11, 1951, Moon and Kaemmerle Associates, on behalf of Metropolitan Mutual, sent a letter to Claude A. Barnett, president of the Associated Negro Press.* This communique urged Barnett to send Metropolitan Mutual a congratulatory statement concerning the January 21, 1951 opening of its new branch office in East St. Louis, Illinois.[26] Barnett's subsequent statement, read at the East St. Louis opening, complimented Metropolitan Mutual for both its expansion into East St. Louis and its historic role as an influential black institution.[27]

To increase the impact of Barnett's favorable assessment of Metropolitan Mutual, Moon and Kaemmerle Associates again contacted Claude A. Barnett in early March 1951. Molly Moon,* after thanking Barnett for his earlier congratulatory statement, expressed Metropolitan Mutual's desire to have Barnett's complimentary statement published in black newspapers serving the Chicago and East St. Louis areas.[28] Barnett's subsequent compliance with Moon's request further publicized Metropolitan Mutual's expansion into East St. Louis, as well as the company's historic role in Bronzeville.

Moon and Kaemmerle's successful efforts, along with such internal accomplishments as an expanded insurance portfolio and a reorganized (and more efficient) administrative structure, resulted in a near tripling of the company's admitted assets between 1947 and 1952 (see table 2–6). Although the corresponding increase in policyholders was not as dramatic, nearly 186,000 black Illinois residents (mainly in Chicago) were policyholders by 1952 (see table 2–7).

Since the Metropolitan Mutual Assurance Company of Chicago was a mutual legal reserve company, policyholders also profited from the company's growth. On June 27, 1949, Metropolitan Mutual's Board of

---

*Claude A. Barnett founded the Associated Negro Press in 1919. The Associated Negro Press, an African American equivalent of United Press International (UPI) and the Associated Press (AP), provided member newspapers with detailed coverage of activities within black communities throughout America.

*Besides her work with Moon and Kaemmerle, Molly Moon is credited with establishing the influential National Urban League Guild in 1942. The guild, an independent fundraising auxiliary of the Urban League, has raised millions of dollars for the NUL. See Darlene Clark Hine, ed., *Black Women in America: An Historical Encyclopedia*, pp. 810–11, 871–74.

TABLE 2–6
Admitted Assets,
Metropolitan Mutual Assurance Company of Chicago,
1947–1952

Year	Admitted Assets
1947	$2,761,282
1948	3,491,036
1949	4,148,371
1950	4,737,552
1951	5,464,020
1952	6,605,359

Source: Minutes, Annual Meetings, Metropolitan Mutual Assurance Company of Chicago, January 19, 1948; January 17, 1949; January 16, 1950; January 15, 1951; January 21, 1952; January 19, 1953.

TABLE 2–7
Number of Policyholders,
Metropolitan Mutual Assurance Company of Chicago,
1947–1952

Year	Policyholders
1947	167,025
1948	181,653
1949	NA
1950	176,186
1951	181,135
1952	185,894

Source: Minutes, Annual Meetings, Metropolitan Mutual Assurance Company of Chicago, January 19, 1948; January 17, 1949; January 15, 1951; January 21, 1952; January 19, 1953.

Directors instituted the firm's first dividend payment schedule for industrial insurance policyholders. Dividends were to issued as follows:

Year Policy Issued	Amount of Dividend
1931 and prior	4 weekly premiums
1932 thru 1936	3 weekly premiums
1937 thru 1941	2 weekly premiums
1942 thru 1946	1 weekly premium[29]

At its January 9, 1950, meeting, the board, likewise, established a dividend program for ordinary insurance policies purchased on or before January 1, 1947.[30] Despite initial uncertainty surrounding the company's reorganization, by the early 1950s the Metropolitan Mutual Assurance Company of Chicago had further established itself as a credible community institution. Although Metropolitan Mutual's embryonic ordinary insurance program started moderately, the company's industrial insurance coverage had become immensely popular. Moreover, MMACC's expansion into East St. Louis, Peoria, and Springfield, along with the new Parkway Dining Room's growing popularity, aided in increasing the company's visibility and stature. Still, while Metropolitan Mutual personnel and policyholders basked in the glow of burgeoning commercial success, an unlikely adversary would soon attempt to spoil the company's celebration.

On January 12, 1951, the Chicago law firm of Eckert, Peterson, and Leeming, on behalf of the Metropolitan Life Insurance Company of New York, filed a complaint against the Metropolitan Mutual Assurance Company of Chicago. Among the charges leveled against Metropolitan Mutual were:

1. As used by the defendant, the defendant's name is deceptively similar to the name of the plaintiff and has given rise, and is likely to give rise in the future, to confusion in the mind of the general public, including policyholders, prospective policyholders, and borrowers, as to the respective identities of the plaintiff and the defendant, and has deceived and is likely in the future to deceive members of the general public into a false belief that the defendant is the plaintiff.

2. The defendant has interfered with and damaged the business of the plaintiff by selling life insurance policies to persons who intend to deal with the plaintiff and not the defendant; the defendant has placed in jeopardy, wrongfully used, and diluted the reputation and good will of the plaintiff which the plaintiff has built up carefully over many years of fair dealing with the public.[31]

To remedy this situation, Metropolitan Life sought the following judgment:

1. The defendant be permanently enjoined and restrained from using the word "Metropolitan" in its corporate title.

2. The defendant be required to account to plaintiff for all profits unjustly obtained by defendant by the wrongful use of the word "Metropolitan" as part of its corporate title.

3. Plaintiff have and recover from defendant the damages sustained by reason of the wrongful acts of the defendant hereinabove alleged, together with the plaintiff's costs and disbursements in this action.[32]

On February 8, 1951, attorneys James B. Cashin and Edward B. Toles, on behalf of Metropolitan Mutual, filed an official response to Metropolitan Life's charges. Among other things, Cashin and Toles contended:

1. Defendant alleges that the complaint of the plaintiff fails to state a cause of action against the defendant since the name "Metropolitan" is generic or descriptive and is accordingly incapable of exclusive appropriation by the plaintiff or any person.

2. Defendant denies that it has by any of its actions confused or will confuse the public into the false belief that the plaintiff and the defendant are one and the same company . . . during all the time of the defendant's existence, its activities have been confined wholly to the State of Illinois and almost exclusively to the County of Cook among people of color, commonly known as Negroes. *Policies of insurance are solicited and sold exclusively on behalf of this defendant by Negro agents. Defendant alleges that the plaintiff does not nor has ever has employed Negro agents to solicit business and risks among Negro people in Chicago and Cook County, Illinois.*[33] (Emphasis mine)

The ensuing case, which the Chicago *Defender* aptly described as a "David and Goliath legal battle,"[34] was obviously important in its own right. Still, an assessment of its significance must necessarily include a survey of the historical relationship between white insurance companies and black consumers before 1951.

As early as 1875, large white insurance companies insured African Americans. During their initial contact with blacks, companies such as the Prudential Insurance Company of Newark and Metropolitan Life of New York offered blacks and whites identical coverage at identical cost.[35] Nevertheless, in March 1881, Prudential, citing an excessive black mortality rate, established a policy whereby blacks paid higher premiums and received less coverage than whites.[36] Other companies soon followed

Prudential's lead and established their own separate and unequal black insurance programs.

Frederick L. Hoffman, Prudential's statistician, was the person responsible for the company's policy change. Although Prudential subsequently denied that racism influenced its policy change toward blacks, a later Hoffman study unequivocally demonstrated the racial overtones of his research.

In 1896, Frederick L. Hoffman published a widely disseminated study entitled *Race Traits and the Tendencies of the American Negro*. Hoffman, alleging Anglo-Saxon superiority, predicted:

> When the ever increasing white population has reached a stage where new conquests are necessary, it will not hesitate to make war upon those races who prove themselves useless factors in the progress of mankind. A race may be interesting, gentle, and hospitable; but if it is not a useful race . . . it is only a matter of time when a downward course must take place . . . that is, a decrease in the population will take place. In the meantime, however, the presence of the colored population is a serious hindrance to the economic progress of the white race.[37]

It appears that Hoffman's premonition concerning the future extinction of African Americans contributed to Prudential's and several other companies subsequent decision to sever all ties with black consumers.[38] This abandonment of black policyholders by white companies assisted the development of black-owned insurance companies.[39]

Despite the furor caused by Hoffman's book, the Metropolitan Life Insurance Company of New York continued to seek black business. Still, Metropolitan Life, according to a company historian, wrote policies ". . . at rates commensurate with mortality experience."[40]

Metropolitan Life, because of its prominence and policy of serving black consumers, attracted a sizable number of African American customers during the early twentieth century. By the late 1920s, a reported 6,500,000 blacks had nearly a billion dollars of insurance in force with the company.[41] Unfortunately, Metropolitan Life, despite the support of black consumers, practiced racial discrimination in investment decisions and hiring.

Although a 1928 investigation of Metropolitan Life revealed a reported $50,000,000 yearly premium income from its black policyholders, this same probe asserted ". . . somehow very little money is available for loans upon colored homes or business buildings."[42] Moreover, as late as

1944, blacks widely criticized Metropolitan Life for its reported intent to bar African Americans from a company-financed $6,000,000 Harlem housing project.[43]

Perhaps the most galling aspect of Metropolitan Life's discriminatory practices was its refusal to hire black agents. Metropolitan Mutual's legal team cited this well-publicized corporate policy to counter Metropolitan Life's suit against the black Chicago company.[44]

Metropolitan Life's suit against Metropolitan Mutual, in retrospect, appears to have been ill-advised from both a legal and a public relations standpoint. Considering Metropolitan Life's refusal to hire black agents, its assertions concerning public confusion as to the identities of the two companies seemed ludicrous. As one Metropolitan Mutual policyholder succinctly stated:

> How foolish! How dumb do they think Negroes are? We know that Negroes cannot sell Metropolitan Life; we know that Metropolitan Life only gives us a second-rate policy. We know that when a Negro agent offers us a first-rate policy under any name it is a Negro company, and that is what hurts Metropolitan Life.[45]

Metropolitan Life's suit against Metropolitan Mutual also appeared mean-spirited. In 1951, the giant Metropolitan Life had more than 40 million policyholders and 50 billion dollars of insurance in force. Metropolitan Mutual, by contrast, had 181,000 policyholders and 50 million dollars of insurance in force.[46] Consequently, Metropolitan Life's suit was a seemingly blatant attempt to destroy a black company that posed little threat to its profitability.

Besides the efforts of Metropolitan Mutual's legal team, black Chicago newspapers joined the fight to "save" the company. On March 13, 1951, the Chicago *Defender* published an article entitled "Metropolitan Mutual—Titan of the Business World," which gave a full-page account of the company's accomplishments. This article, among other things, revealed that Metropolitan Mutual had recently been rated as "excellent" and "worthy of public confidence" by Dunne's International Insurance Reports, the world's largest policyholders reporting service.[47]

The July 7, 1951, issue of the Chicago *Courier* offered an even more complimentary assessment of Metropolitan Mutual. The *Courier*, which had become a strong competitor of the *Defender*, published a two-page feature entitled "Metropolitan Mutual: A Monument to Integrity." The *Courier*, after surveying MMACC's achievements, concluded:

A thrilling physical sight in its beautiful plant, the significance of Metropolitan Mutual lies even deeper than its stone and steel foundation—the
significance is in the economic power that lies within the Negro race
when men of integrity and business training take over the leadership of
that power.[48]

The subsequent trial basically upheld Metropolitan Mutual's defense.
Still, it did substantiate Metropolitan Life's assertions that blacks often
referred to Metropolitan Mutual simply as "Metropolitan." A November
7, 1952, consent decree ultimately settled the conflict over the use of
"Metropolitan." This document ordered the Metropolitan Mutual Assurance Company to change its name to Chicago Metropolitan Mutual
Assurance Company within a year. The court also directed Metropolitan
Life to pay the black Chicago company $6,000 to cover the legal cost of
this move.[49]

Metropolitan Mutual personnel and policyholders hailed the November 7, 1952, consent decree as a victory.[50] Not only did it deny damages to
Metropolitan Life, but Metropolitan Mutual maintained the legal right
to continue using "Metropolitan" in its company name. The widespread
publicity given the trial, moreover, placed Metropolitan Mutual in the
enviable position as a recognized fighter for African American economic
progress.

Unfortunately, a sense of grief coexisted with the euphoria surrounding the disposition of Metropolitan Life's suit. Attorney James B. Cashin,
who led the company's legal battle, died on July 11, 1952.[51] Cashin, who
had represented the company in court since 1930, was a popular figure
known for his thoughtful orations at the conclusion of company annual
meetings. He, along with other deceased company pioneers Fred W.
Lewing and Rev. Mansfield Edward Bryant Peck, were honored with a
moment of silence at the January 19, 1953, annual meeting.[52]

The year 1952 witnessed not only the favorable settlement of Metropolitan Life's suit, but marked the twenty-fifth anniversary of the Robert
A. Cole–led company. To celebrate this significant milestone, Metropolitan Mutual sponsored a variety of events during the year.

In March, Metropolitan Mutual opened a branch office at 2350 Madison Street, a site located in the heart of Chicago's West Side African
American enclave.[53] The subsequent development of this territory enhanced the company's financial situation.

December 1952 represented an especially festive period for the company. On December 22–23, Metropolitan Mutual held an open house at

its home office. Among the souvenirs presented to visitors was a pamphlet entitled "A Dream Come True: The Story of the MMACC, 1927–1952." This publication summarized the company's history and evaluated its current operations. Metropolitan Mutual's growing mortgage loan program and its sponsorship of the Parkway Ballroom and Dining Room were given special emphasis.[54]

A banquet held at the Parkway Ballroom on December 29, 1952, marked the grand finale of the company's twenty-fifth anniversary celebration. Dr. Charles S. Johnson, president of Fisk University, was the keynote speaker of this affair. Johnson praised Metropolitan Mutual for succeeding in the face of adversity. Robert A. Cole, before Johnson's keynote address, delivered a speech that outlined the company's growth into one of black America's most prestigious companies. Moreover, Cole, at the conclusion of his remarks, presented Dr. Johnson a check for $3,200 to be used as a company-sponsored four-year scholarship to Fisk.[55]

Besides the speeches given by Robert A. Cole and Dr. Charles S. Johnson, Metropolitan Mutual's twenty-fifth anniversary banquet featured congratulatory messages from Illinois Governor Adlai E. Stevenson, Chicago Mayor Martin J. Kennelley, and U.S. Senators (from Illinois) Everett Dirksen and Paul Douglas. Also, greetings from survivors of persons buried by the old Metropolitan Funeral System Association were graciously acknowledged.[56]

As the soon-to-be Chicago Metropolitan Mutual Assurance Company entered its twenty-sixth year of operation, it could be justifiably proud of its accomplishments. The company, despite numerous obstacles, had somehow survived. Still, while there was cause for celebration, business endeavor remained an ongoing process. Thus, maintaining the momentum gained from twenty-five years of service became the company's top priority.

III

THE CHICAGO METROPOLITAN
MUTUAL ASSURANCE COMPANY,
1953–1957

Metropolitan Mutual's legal battle with Metropolitan Life catapulted this black Chicago insurance company into the national spotlight. While such publicity had indisputable benefits, it also created additional expectations. Consequently, the renamed Chicago Metropolitan Mutual Assurance Company's initial years were characterized by an accelerated attempt to operate as a modern corporation. These efforts, which generated additional positive exposure, proved successful. Yet just as the company appeared poised to expand its influence in the insurance industry it endured a major scandal, the death of its president, and a strike that forever changed the way company personnel related to each other.

Company officials, in accordance with the November 7, 1952, consent decree, completed the task of changing Metropolitan Mutual's corporate name in early March 1953.[1] Moreover, the Board of Directors used the occasion of assuming a new name to modify and expand company operations.

The first step toward corporate reorganization took place at the April 13, 1953, board meeting. Among other matters, the Chicago Metropolitan board repealed all existing company by-laws and inaugurated new ones. Perhaps the most significant characteristic of the new by-laws was their definitive listing of the duties and powers of both the Board of Directors and individual company officers. These new provisions further clarified company procedures.[2]

The CMMAC Board of Directors instituted additional changes at its April 5, 1954, meeting. Prompted by a decrease in premium income from the company's chief Chicago territory (see table 3–1), the board agreed to take the necessary steps to expand operations into Indiana, Missouri,

TABLE 3–1
Weekly Premium Income,
Chicago Metropolitan Mutual Assurance Company,
1953–1954

	1953	1954
Chicago	$57,123	$56,689
Downstate	6,908	7,583
Total	64,031	64,272

Source: Minutes, Annual Meetings, Chicago Metropolitan Mutual Assurance Company, January 18, 1954, January 17, 1955.

and Ohio.[3] After deciding to commence interstate expansion, the board then sought to convince Chicago Metropolitan personnel and policy-holders of its potential benefits.

At the company's January 17, 1955, annual meeting, President Robert A. Cole asserted that interstate expansion would increase CMMAC's weekly premium income by $10,000 during 1955.[4] Moreover, First Vice-President Thomas P. Harris contended that Chicago Metropolitan's growth into neighboring states would result in new opportunities for employee advancement.[5]

Although Robert A. Cole's prediction concerning 1955 premium income growth subsequently fell a bit short (see table 3–2), Thomas P. Harris proved to be a more accurate prophet. Interstate expansion immediately provided skilled Chicago Metropolitan personnel an op-portunity to assume additional responsibilities and rewards. One such person was Lynn Langston, Jr., the agent credited with leading the campaign to build Chicago Metropolitan's new Indiana territory.

Lynn Langston joined CMMAC (then Metropolitan Mutual) as an agent in 1948. Before entering the insurance industry, he had a success-ful sales career with the Fuller Products Company.[6] In early 1955, Langston and other "builders" began the process of opening up Indiana and they secured contacts in East Chicago, Gary, and South Bend. Similar to previous "builders" who established downstate Illinois territo-ries, Langston and his cohorts forged links with Indiana black ministers. Langston's successful coordination of the project resulted in several promotions within Chicago Metropolitan's Agency Department.[7]

Jesse L. Moman was another "builder" destined to advance within the company. Moman, who later served as vice-president/claims director,

TABLE 3–2
Weekly Premium Income,
Chicago Metropolitan Mutual Assurance Company,
1954–1955

	1954	1955
Chicago	$56,689	$60,087
Downstate	7,583	7,536
Indiana	—	2,539
Missouri	—	450
Total	64,272	70,612

Source: Minutes, Annual Meeting, Chicago Metropolitan Mutual Assurance Company, January 16, 1956.

received his first big "break" during the mid-1950s when assigned to assist in the campaign to open up St. Louis, Missouri. There, as in downstate Illinois and Indiana, the assistance of local African American ministers helped ensure CMMAC's success.[8]

Chicago Metropolitan's initial thrust as an interstate corporation marked a true milestone in its history. The once struggling burial association could now assert that it was a regional, as well as a Chicago and Illinois insurance company. Considering the relative dearth of similar black business success stories during this period, the Chicago Metropolitan Mutual Assurance Company (and especially Robert A. Cole) attracted considerable media attention.

Even before CMMAC's expansion into neighboring states, *Ebony* magazine saw fit to present the company's achievements to a nationwide audience. *Ebony*, in its January 1953 issue, saluted the (then) Metropolitan Mutual's twenty-fifth anniversary. Noting the company's humble origins, *Ebony* proudly asserted:

> Founded in a tiny, overcrowded basement office in 1927, Metropolitan is now housed in one of the most impressive structures ever built and owned by Negroes. Metropolitan's home office building on South Parkway has become one of the showplaces of Chicago's South Side.[9]

Besides surveying the company's history and current operations, the January 1953 *Ebony* article praised the efforts of President Robert A. Cole. Cole, once viewed with scorn (by some) because of his gambling activities, appeared to *Ebony* readers as "King Cole," a self-made man who succeeded despite a limited educational background.[10]

Both Robert A. Cole's and Chicago Metropolitan's stature among African Americans received further enhancement when Cole's semi-autobiographical essay, entitled "How I Made a Million," appeared in *Ebony*'s September 1954 issue. Ostensibly written to inspire achievement among black youth, Cole declared that if someone with his background could achieve success, any black could.[11]

Along with the black media's favorable depiction of both CMMAC and Robert A. Cole, white publications also took notice of the company and its president. On July 9, 1955, the Chicago *Tribune* published an extensive article entitled "200,000 Trust Robert A. Cole with Their Savings." The following excerpt conveys the tone of this piece:

> The modern building at 4455 South Parkway, which houses this business (CMMAC) stands as a testimony to a man who demonstrated vision and daring in the best rags-to-riches tradition. More important, Cole operates one of the largest aggregations of private capital ever assembled in a single Chicago enterprise directed by a Negro.[12]

The July 1955 Chicago *Tribune* article appeared to represent yet another milestone in CMMAC's corporate history. While Bronzeville residents had long been aware of the company's activities, this *Tribune* coverage introduced thousands of white Chicagoans to the Chicago Metropolitan Mutual Assurance Company. Unfortunately, the warm breezes of adulation and praise soon gave way to the cold winds of scandal.

On December 2, 1955, Chicago police arrested Mary F. Cole, the wife of Robert A. Cole, for her purported role in an extortion ring. Mrs. Cole, along with two accomplices, reportedly extorted (at gunpoint) over $20,000 from CMMAC officials Horace G. Hall and James D. Grantham.[13] According to a knowledgeable informant, Hall and Grantham apparently elicited Mrs. Cole's ire because they opposed her bid for Chicago Metropolitan board membership.

Mary F. Cole, before her arrest, appeared prestigious in her own right. Mrs. Cole, a licensed mortician, was the first black to serve on the faculty of Chicago's Worsham College of Mortuary Science.[14] Besides her teaching duties, Mary Cole served as assistant manager of her husband's Metropolitan Funeral Parlors.[15]

Mary Cole's arrest appeared to have been the culmination of events that had disturbed Robert A. Cole for some time. Evidence suggests that while Robert A. Cole's (public) stature reached a zenith of recognition and admiration, his home life had plummeted to the depths of despair. Chief among Cole's concerns was his wife's growing extravagance and increased attachment to her chauffeur, Robert (Kelly) Rose.[16] Still, Mary Cole's alleged attempt to extort funds from CMMAC officials* moved the Coles' marital problems into the realm of public scrutiny. Ironically, Chicago Met's recently enhanced visibility transformed Mrs. Cole's arrest into a scandal of major proportions.

Fortunately, for the company, the Mary Cole debacle did not have an adverse effect on CMMAC's prestige and profitability (see table 3–3). But for Robert A. Cole, public disclosure of his marital problems proved to be enormously embarrassing. The robust "King Cole" of Chicago, a man noted for his jovial good nature and genuine love of people, soon became a sickly recluse. Until his death on July 27, 1956, Cole avoided such important company functions as the January 16, 1956, annual meeting and all 1956 Board of Directors meetings.[17]

Despite distractions caused by Mary F. Cole, CMMAC's Board of Directors (minus Cole) continued the company's thrust toward corporate expansion coupled with greater efficiency. The board, at its December 12, 1955, meeting, approved the following significant resolutions: (1) the company's Board of Directors would be increased from three to seven members; (2) the establishment of the official position, chairman of the board; and (3) the creation of an executive committee consisting of the chairman of the board, the president, and the secretary.[18] The board also agreed to designate the first vice-president as an executive committee member if the president and the chairman of the board were the same person.[19] These actions resulted in James D. Grantham, George S. Harris, Melvin McNairy, and James W. Tyler joining Robert A. Cole, Thomas P. Harris, and Horace G. Hall on the Chicago Metropolitan board.[20]

The company's new board members represented a variety of backgrounds and experiences. James D. Grantham and Melvin McNairy were company pioneers whose professional growth paralleled CMMAC's historical development. George S. Harris was a newer member of the Chicago Met "family." Still, his successful administration of both the

---

*Mary Cole subsequently escaped conviction on this charge because evidence secured through a wiretap (ordered by Robert A. Cole) could not be used in court. See Associated Negro Press, News Release, August 1, 1956, p. 24, Claude A. Barnett Papers, Chicago Historical Society.

TABLE 3–3
**Selected Characteristics of Company Operations,
Chicago Metropolitan Mutual Assurance Company,
1955–1956**

	1955	*1956*
Total Admitted Assets	$9,189,498	$10,116,706
Weekly Premium Income		
Chicago	$60,087	$61,424
Downstate	7,536	8,053
Indiana	2,539	4,610
Missouri	450	1,910
Total	$70,612	$75,997
Number of Policies in Force	226,781	234,967

Source: Minutes, Annual Meeting, Chicago Metropolitan Mutual Assurance Company, January 21, 1957.

Parkway Amusement Corporation and CMMAC's Real Estate & Investment Department enhanced Harris's importance within the company. Finally, James Willard Tyler's selection to the CMMAC board demonstrated an implicit policy to choose future board members not only on the basis of longevity, but on the basis of their potential contribution to company well-being.

After Tyler, who grew up in Chicago, graduated from Fisk University in 1942 he joined the old Metropolitan Funeral System Association as an agent. It appears that Tyler's college training in bookkeeping and accounting, along with his exemplary record within the company, contributed to his 1955 selection to the CMMAC board. Moreover, after assuming this promotion Tyler also became company comptroller.[21]

Besides the expansion of the Chicago Metropolitan Board of Directors from three to seven members, the actions taken at the board's December 12, 1955, meeting also led to a dramatic change in the company's day-to-day administration. One of the resolutions passed at this board meeting created the position of chairman of the board. Robert A. Cole, considering his long tenure as president, appeared the obvious choice for this largely ceremonial position. Still, in light of Cole's serious marital problems, along with his advancing age (he was 73), remaining board members were faced with a dilemma over Cole's continuing as company president. On the one hand, Cole's fellow board members loved and respected him. Yet, conversely, since the president's responsibilities included coordinating the company's daily operations, he needed to be as free as possible from outside distractions. Cole's absence from the important January 16, 1956, annual meeting made the board's choice between sentimentality and sound business principles much easier. At the board meeting held immediately following the January 16, 1956, annual meeting, board members designated Robert A. Cole as chairman of the board and Thomas P. Harris as president.[22]

In addition to the election of various company officials, including long-time employees Charles L. Bell and Zeb Perkins as vice-president/cashier and assistant secretary/claims manager, respectively, the January 16, 1956, board meeting addressed the issue of employee recruitment and retention.[23] During the company's first 29 years, Chicago Metropolitan, along with other black-owned firms, provided a sizable percentage of the clerical and professional positions available to black Chicagoans. Yet, by the mid-1950s, several mainstream Chicago corporations began to abolish the historic occupational discrimination practiced against Bronzeville citizens. Consequently, blacks now had an opportunity to work downtown in capacities other than janitor, elevator operator, or cleaning woman.[24]

To help insure retention of its skilled personnel and to attract additional employees, the CMMAC board gave new President Thomas P. Harris the power to grant special seniority status to both current and future personnel.[25] This action attests to the fact that, as early as 1956, black companies viewed the impending integration of the white-owned corporate labor force as potentially damaging to their operations.

Despite several important measures passed by the CMMAC board in 1956, Robert A. Cole's July 27 death represented the most noteworthy event of the year. For nearly twenty-nine years, Cole, along with other company pioneers, had built a small burial association into one of the country's top black businesses. Although some criticized Cole's penchant for gambling, his willingness to take risks contributed to Chicago Metropolitan's success. Moreover, Cole's greatest legacy may have been his genuine concern for black Chicago's working class.

Robert A. Cole, unlike many business executives, maintained touch with the "man on the street." Because of his own limited educational and social background, Cole felt a special affinity with CMMAC's overwhelmingly working class constituency. Throughout his tenure as president,

Cole made a point of being accessible to policyholders. Even later in life, while universally lauded for his accomplishments, it was not uncommon to observe "King Cole" strolling through the streets of Bronzeville exchanging pleasantries with old friends and passersby. Consequently, much of black Chicago, along with Chicago Metropolitan personnel and policyholders, mourned Robert A. Cole's death.

After Cole's impressive July 31, 1956, funeral, which included such distinguished pallbearers as John H. Johnson, publisher of *Ebony,* and John H. Sengstacke, editor of the Chicago *Defender,*[26] the Chicago Metropolitan Mutual Assurance Company entered a new phase in its history. Yet, because President Thomas P. Harris had coordinated company operations since January 1956, the subsequent transition went relatively smoothly.

Shortly after Cole's death, Chicago Metropolitan's Board of Directors sought a means to properly honor both him and Fred Lewing's legacy. At its November 19, 1956, meeting, the CMMAC board agreed to install a bronze plaque honoring Cole and Lewing in the home office lobby. In addition, the board resolved to include the names of subsequently deceased board members on that plaque.[27]

Besides a commemorative plaque, CMMAC sought to honor the memory of Cole and Lewing by establishing scholarships in their names. In April 1957, the board designated Fisk University to coordinate the Robert A. Cole Scholarship.[28] In June, the board chose Roosevelt University in Chicago to administer the Fred W. Lewing Scholarship.[29]

Despite actions taken to honor Cole and Lewing's legacy, Robert A. Cole's death forced Chicago Metropolitan to focus upon its future. At the January 21, 1957, annual meeting, policyholders chose Dr. Edward Beasley to replace Robert A. Cole on the Board of Directors. This meeting also featured an important speech by President Thomas P. Harris concerning the post-Cole Chicago Metropolitan Mutual Assurance Company. Harris declared that despite the prestige and visibility of CMMAC's past and present Board of Directors, rank and file personnel were equally, if not more, responsible for the company's dramatic growth. Consequently, if Chicago Metropolitan hoped to continue to prosper, each employee must realize:

> We are not only selling insurance, computing figures, settling claims, and administering the assets of the company, we are also—all of us— engaged in a public relations job. Every officer, every employee, of this company is an ambassador for the company. . . . To the man in the street,

to the potential policyholder coming into our offices or encountering
you off the premises, you represent the company. His impression of
Chicago Metropolitan is based in large measure on the impression you
make on him.[30]

Although the meeting applauded Harris's uplifting message, 1957
proved to be the most traumatic year in Chicago Metropolitan's history.
An agent strike during the summer adversely affected company morale
and profitability. It appeared the much-heralded expansion into neighboring states contributed directly to the troubles of 1957.

Beginning in 1955, expansion into Indiana and Missouri were given
top priority. To stimulate the development of these territories, agents in
these locales received special monetary incentives. As the Illinois Department of Insurance noted in its March 15, 1957 examination of CMMAC,
agents working outside of Illinois earned collection commissions rang-
ing from 20 to 50 percent of the first $100 of weekly premium collections
and 20 percent of collections over $100 weekly.[31] These figures compared
to the 15 percent weekly collection commission, which represented a 5
percent decrease, earned by agents working in Chicago.[32] Considering
the wide discrepancy in commissions paid to Chicago agents and agents
elsewhere, the Chicago agents' protest appeared justifiable.

Present and retired Chicago Metropolitan personnel who remember
this period agree that, had Robert A. Cole been alive, the 1957 agent
strike would probably not have taken place.[33] Cole, throughout his
tenure as president, accorded company agents considerable respect and
consideration. He correctly realized that an insurance company prospers
or declines because of its agents' performance. Thus, Cole made keeping
his agents happy a top priority (see chapter 5).

Thomas P. Harris apparently did not share Cole's special sensitivity
toward agents. Besides Melvin McNairy (then agency director), the rest
of the CMMAC board shared President Harris's seeming lack of concern
about Chicago agents' grievances.[34] Consequently, Chicago-based agents,
believing they had no other recourse, spent the summer of 1957 carrying
picket signs instead of servicing their debits. This action, resulting in a
decline of both premium income (see table 3–4) and company morale,
represented a severe breach within the previously close Chicago Metropolitan "family" (see chapter 5).

On August 6, 1957, after weeks of sometimes bitter negotiations, the
CMMAC Board of Directors came to terms with Building Service Employees' International Union Local 189 (representing the agents). Among

TABLE 3–4
Weekly Premium Income,
Chicago Metropolitan Mutual Assurance Company,
1956–1957

	1956	*1957*
Chicago	$61,424	$54,713
Downstate	8,053	7,069
Indiana	4,610	3,984
Missouri	1,910	1,943
Total	$75,997	$67,709

Source: Minutes, Annual Meeting, Chicago Metropolitan Mutual Assurance Company, January 20, 1958.

the major provisions of the agreed-upon four-year contract were: (1) designation of CMMAC as a union shop—all agents had to join the union as a condition for employment; (2) establishment of a uniform commission structure for agents regardless of where they worked; and (3) creation of formalized vacation and sick leave benefits for agents.[35]

Another important consequence of the strike was Melvin McNairy's dismissal as agency director and the subsequent hiring of Lorenzo D. Jones.[36] McNairy, later re-assigned to the post of public relations director,[37] reportedly elicited the ire of President Thomas P. Harris because of his sympathetic views concerning the striking agents.[38] While the CMMAC board primarily brought in Jones because of his "no nonsense" approach to agency administration, he ultimately demonstrated other skills which revolutionized Chicago Metropolitan's Agency Department.

Before joining CMMAC in September 1957, Lorenzo D. Jones, a native of Henderson, Kentucky, had successful managerial stints with several other African American insurance companies.[39] Still, despite his impressive credentials Jones faced a difficult task at Chicago Metropolitan. Despite the strike's settlement a residue of mistrust remained between the company's management team and agency force. Jones himself contributed to the tension. Unlike the affable Melvin McNairy, who motivated agents with friendly encouragement,[40] Lorenzo Jones was a stern taskmaster, reminiscent of the late Fred W. Lewing. Fortunately, Jones possessed expertise that ultimately earned him the respect, if not the affection, of CMMAC's agency force.

On November 22, 1957, less than two months after joining CMMAC, Lorenzo D. Jones submitted a far-reaching report to the Board of

Directors. This document began by asserting that CMMAC faced the
major challenges of rebuilding Agency Department morale and over-
coming a sizable decrease in premium income. Jones proposed to
address these problems by:

1. Maintaining a closer relationship with individual agents and all field
   personnel.

2. Publishing a weekly Agency bulletin which will reflect the past week's
   operation to the entire field force. Such a publication will hopefully
   motivate agents as well as dispel charges of favoritism in promotions
   through this spotlighting of achievement.

3. Developing specific operational instructional manuals reflecting
   company policy.

4. Advising agents to place equal emphasis on Weekly Premium,
   Monthly Premium, and Ordinary Insurance.[41]

Along with proposals concerning rank and file agents, Jones's November 22, 1957, report also recommended an overhaul of the Agency
Department's administrative structure. Among Jones's tentative objectives for 1958 were:

1. To complete in its entirety the branch office system of company
   operations with the decentralization of agency functions at the
   Home Office and to arrange for each unit of company business to be
   served by a branch office that will be responsible for growth, cost,
   and proper policyholder service of this business.

2. To institute an intensive training program for branch office managers and to allocate such responsibilities as increase quotas, cost
   factors and collection quotas to these units as a measure of branch
   office efficiency.[42]

To facilitate these objectives, Jones recommended that Agency Department personnel hold a branch office management training conference
on December 17–18, 1957. Moreover, Jones advised the board that such
a conference should be held, for purposes of evaluation and ongoing
training, four times a year.[43] Finally, to properly conduct the proposed
management and field training program, Lorenzo D. Jones urged the
company to purchase the appropriate instructional materials.[44]

Jones's far-reaching proposals, approved by the CMMAC board on
November 27, 1957,[45] culminated the thrust toward modern corporate
administration begun in the late 1940s. The company's reorganization
from a burial association to a legal reserve company necessitated the

initial movement toward corporate power-sharing. Similarly, CMMAC's mid-1950s expansion into neighboring states resulted in an even greater diffusion of administrative responsibility. Jones's plans to institute autonomous agency districts in Illinois, Indiana, and Missouri, along with the recent expansion of the Board of Directors from three to seven members, signaled the extension and entrenchment of a new corporate bureaucratic structure.

Although the term "bureaucracy" has become a value-laden word with sometimes negative connotations, CMMAC's implementation of an expanded chain of command represented sound business strategy. Still, while CMMAC's expanded executive team sought internal means to enhance efficiency and profitability, external forces (beyond their control) were beginning to offer another challenge to company survival.

African Americans applauded the United States Supreme Court's May 17, 1954, decision in the *Brown vs. Board of Education of Topeka, Kansas* case. Yet this landmark ruling represented a distinct challenge to Chicago Metropolitan and other black businesses. In his Presidential Report at CMMAC's January 20, 1958, annual meeting, Thomas P. Harris examined desegregation's potential impact on company operations. Harris, after admitting that CMMAC had prospered within a segregated economy, asserted that Chicago Metropolitan could, indeed, meet the challenge integration posed. Specifically, he declared "we will be able to walk, even run, without the crutch of segregation."[46]

After Harris's remarks concerning Chicago Metropolitan's future, the January 20, 1958, annual meeting moved from the Parkway Ballroom to the first floor lobby. Here, Rev. Richard Keller, CMMAC's chaplain, presided over a litany service which featured the unveiling of commemorative plaques honoring Robert A. Cole and Fred W. Lewing. Although this ceremony appeared to represent the end of one era and the beginning of another, subsequent events demonstrated the permanence of Cole and Lewing's legacy.

Despite Thomas P. Harris's optimism concerning CMMAC's future, the black working-class constituency, cultivated by Cole and Lewing, remained Chicago Met's primary market during the 1960s and succeeding decades (see chapter 6). Another significant legacy of Robert A. Cole and Fred W. Lewing was their belief that Chicago Metropolitan should contribute to the social, as well as the economic needs of the black community. Consequently, the company's historical importance extended beyond the confines of the insurance business.

IV

THE CHICAGO METROPOLITAN ASSURANCE COMPANY AS AN AFRICAN AMERICAN COMMUNITY INSTITUTION, 1927–1957

Besides providing economical insurance coverage to Chicago's black community, the old Metropolitan Funeral System Association (and its later derivatives) sought to exert a positive influence on other sectors of African American life. Robert A. Cole, sometimes using personal gambling winnings, promoted the company's involvement in a myriad of community enhancement activities. Ironically, at the time of his death, black Chicagoans, optimistic about the implications of racial integration, had begun to abandon some of the community-based institutions that Cole and his company had created or supported.

When Robert A. Cole took control of the Metropolitan Funeral System Association in 1927, the company had been exclusively concerned with providing low-cost funerals to black Chicago residents. Cole, however, believed MFSA should expand its influence in Bronzeville. Fred W. Lewing, Cole's chief lieutenant, shared this view. Consequently, the Metropolitan Funeral System Association, while continuing to provide low-cost burials, made an early commitment to funding a variety of community improvement activities.

Cole and Lewing's backgrounds help explain their desire for a diversified MFSA. Both men, before their affiliation with the Metropolitan Funeral System Association, had extensive contact with mainstream American society. Cole had observed firsthand the amenities available to whites during several years as a Pullman porter. Lewing, one of few blacks during this period to grow up on Chicago's North Side, also knew of the superior goods and services available to whites in early twentieth-century America. Thus Cole and Lewing, because of their experiences, apparently viewed MFSA as a means to undertake a broader racial mission. In the tradition of the "Race Man," as described by Cayton and Drake in their classic study *Black Metropolis,* Cole and Lewing felt compelled to provide Bronzeville residents with a variety of services and facilities comparable to those offered whites.[1] Moreover, subsequent company-sponsored community enhancement projects sought to give black Chicagoans the same courtesy and consideration that Cole had given to white train passengers (as a Pullman porter) and Lewing had dispensed to white customers when he owned an exclusive North Side barbershop. Ultimately, Cole and Lewing's attitude toward Bronzeville residents resulted in an enhancement of both MFSA's (and its derivatives') corporate image and profitability.

The Metropolitan Funeral System Association's first significant community enhancement project was a joint venture with Jack Leroy Cooper, a black show-business veteran. The company's relationship with Cooper offered a prime example of a community-minded stimulus for black economic development.

When Jack L. Cooper's "The All Negro Hour" made its November 3, 1929, debut on Chicago radio station WSBC, it marked a true milestone in African American history. Created to counteract mainstream radio's stereotypical depiction of black life, this variety show, which included comedy, musical, and religious vignettes, marked the beginning of the black radio industry.[2] Still, while Cooper had created a format that allowed African Americans to control on-the-air proceedings, white technicians at WSBC continued to direct behind-the-scenes operations. Consequently, Cooper felt compelled to secure a black-staffed recording studio in Bronzeville, thereby, making "The All Negro Hour" an absolute reality.[3]

To accomplish this goal, Cooper sought the support of Bronzeville businessmen. Unfortunately, because of the worsening Depression, the years 1929–1930 were not an opportune time to request venture capital from black Chicago businessmen. Yet when Cooper nearly abandoned his quest for a black Chicago recording studio, Robert A. Cole and Fred W. Lewing agreed to assist him.[4]

MFSA granted Cooper virtual freedom in planning, constructing, and equipping the proposed studio. The completed facility, located at the Metropolitan Funeral System Association's new headquarters at 418 E. 47th Street, proved beneficial to both Cooper and MFSA. Because of the company's direct involvement with "The All Negro Hour"'s growing success, MFSA's stature within Bronzeville grew. In 1931, the company, under Jack L. Cooper's supervision, sponsored a program entitled "The All Negro Children's Hour." This program, similar to "The All Negro Hour," represented a milestone in radio programming.[5]

At the same time the Metropolitan Funeral System Association made an important contribution to the embryonic black radio industry, company officials were independently engaged in another entertainment-related project. In October 1930, Robert A. Cole, Fred W. Lewing, Horace G. Hall, Ahmad A. Rayner, and Edith Lautier, along with Bronzeville journalists Caswell W. Crews and Henry N. Bacon, formed Fireside Publications, Inc. They created this corporation, whose offices were also at MFSA's new 418 E. 47th Street headquarters, to publish the *Bronzeman* magazine.[6]

According to Abby and Ronald Johnson, authors of *Propaganda and Aesthetics: The Literary Politics of Afro-American Magazines in the Twentieth Century,* the *Bronzeman* was one of the most successful black popular magazines during the 1930s.[7] The Johnsons defined a black popular magazine as one that:

> . . . tried to entertain, rather than instruct or lead the larger Afro-American reading public. . . . In pursuit of this aim, black popular magazines featured light fiction, including true confession stories, success stories, gossip columns, and discussions of fashion, homemaking, and sports.[8]

The *Bronzeman* generally followed that format but also attempted to do more than merely entertain.

Racial advancement in education, employment, and business were among the serious topics addressed by the *Bronzeman*. One of the magazine's earliest features was "The *Bronzeman* School Directory." This column, promoted as ". . . one of the *Bronzeman*'s many ways of serving the Negro family,"[9] cited educational opportunities at such institutions as the Hampton Institute, Tuskegee University, Fisk University, and Meharry Medical College.[10] Besides offering a comprehensive listing of black colleges and universities throughout America, the magazine established a free counseling service where potential students and their parents could obtain detailed information about specific institutions.[11]

Along with the *Bronzeman*'s promotion of African American educational achievement, the magazine proudly chronicled the advancement of blacks in the workplace. The June 1931 issue, for instance, featured an article entitled "When Opportunity Knocked, the Negro Girl of Chicago Was at Home." This report described the successful entry of Bronzeville women into clerical positions at Chicago retail stores, Illinois Bell, and Commonwealth Edison.[12]

The subject of black economic development received considerable attention in the *Bronzeman*. Considering that businessmen, led by Robert A. Cole, financed the magazine, this should not be surprising. Still, the *Bronzeman,* rather than merely praise black businessmen, sought to stimulate black business development by rewarding progressive African American enterprise with favorable publicity. The magazine's May 1932 inauguration of its "Certificate of Merit" illustrated this policy. This award, established to highlight the accomplishments of black commercial enterprises focused on:

> . . . the excellence of the equipment and stock, courteous treatment of customers and conspicuous service to the community, making the recipient deserving of the support of the public. Our hope is that these awards will encourage and stimulate business generally as well as acquaint the public with the existence of enterprises operated by the group which feature quality and service.[13]

Mr. R. S. Andrews, the *Bronzeman*'s sales representative, traveled to fourteen cities throughout the United States between May and September 1932.[14] His mission was to survey the status of black business development in these locales and to confer the magazine's "Certificate of Merit" upon deserving enterprises. A hardware store in Oklahoma City, Oklahoma; a dry goods store in Birmingham, Alabama; a beauty shop in Memphis, Tennessee; and a motorist association in Chicago were among the businesses subsequently honored by the *Bronzeman.* Of the twenty-seven "Certificates of Merit" awarded, fourteen went to enterprises owned by men and thirteen went to female entrepreneurs.[15]

The *Bronzeman,* at the conclusion of this five-month investigation, asserted that the "Certificate of Merit" campaign was an overwhelming success. The magazine, by conferring these awards publicly, contended that it contributed to a marked increase in the trade of those honored.[16]

Despite the *Bronzeman*'s optimism concerning its role as a promoter of black business development, the worsening Depression led to its own demise in 1933. As the discretionary income of African Americans decreased, the *Bronzeman*'s $0.10 monthly cost apparently became prohibitive. *Abbott's Monthly,** the other major Depression-era black popular magazine, also ceased publication in 1933 because of worsening economic conditions.[17]

While the *Bronzeman* frequently examined such serious issues as African American economic development, purely entertaining features, such as those cited by the Johnsons, formed the bulk of the magazine's format. Significantly, the *Bronzeman,* along with other Depression-era publications (both black and white), offered readers a literary escape from a depressing reality.

Unlike *Abbott's Monthly,* which featured such famous black writers as Langston Hughes, Richard Wright, and Chester Himes, the *Bronzeman* promoted obscure writers whose contributions appear to have been the pinnacle of their literary careers.*[18] The *Bronzeman* also asked readers to submit articles, poems, and short stories for publication. Still, the magazine's "Letters to the Editor" section, entitled "Bouquets and Bombshells," featured favorable reaction to the magazine from such diverse locales as White Plains, New York, Birmingham, Alabama, and Monrovia, Liberia (West Africa).[19]

The *Bronzeman*'s regular entertainment features included "True Confession" stories, a gossip column entitled "A Letter from Hollywood," a children's page named "The Junior Bronzeman," and a "Bronze Beauties" pictorial section.[20] The *Bronzeman*'s entertainment features, along with articles on serious subjects, catered to a diversity of interests within the African American community.

The *Bronzeman,* besides reflecting the various reading tastes among blacks, regularly addressed the issue of employment (something the majority of Depression-era blacks were concerned with). Working persons of all races were increasingly anxious about growing joblessness during the early 1930s. The *Bronzeman,* in response to this national calamity, sought to provide its readers with employment opportunities.

---

*Robert S. Abbott, editor of the influential Chicago *Defender,* published *Abbott's Monthly.*

*Although the October 1931 *Bronzeman* predicted that regular contributors William T. Smith, Art Naylor, Ruby Berkeley Goodwin, Neale Jackson, Edward H. Lawson, Jr., Lonnie Olga Ricard, and Captain William A. Palmer would ". . . go down in journalistic history as great," none of these individuals are listed in such publications as *Selected Black Authors: An Illustrated Bio-Bibliography* (1977), or *Living Black Authors: A Biographical Directory* (1973). Still, the publication *Black American Writers Past and Present: A Biographical and Bibliographical Dictionary, Volume I* (1975), did list Ruby Berkeley Goodwin on page 329. It noted that she served as a publicist and secretary to actress Hattie McDaniel from 1936 to 1952 and published an autobiography, *It's Good to Be Black,* in 1953.

The August 1931 *Bronzeman,* for instance, featured a prominent advertisement that stated:

> We Welcome and Pay for Stories of adventure, mystery, and love filled with lively dialogue and interestingly told. True stories that convey a helpful message. . . . Articles dealing with Negro life in all its phases accompanied by photographs. . . . Attractive pictures for the Bronze Beauty Page . . . here's an Opportunity To Turn Your Spare Time Into Money.[21]

The *Bronzeman*'s subsequent use of unknown and raw talent diminished the magazine's literary quality. Yet, this policy proved beneficial to both the *Bronzeman* and its artistic readers. The magazine saved money during harsh economic times by employing unknown writers instead of higher-priced professionals. Moreover, talented unknowns were provided an opportunity to supplement their incomes.

Besides providing opportunities for aspiring black writers and photographers, the *Bronzeman* established a program whereby individuals could earn money through subscription sales. The magazine, similar to the Metropolitan Funeral System Association's "open door" agent hiring policy during the Depression, welcomed anyone willing to try their hand at commission sales.[22]

Despite the *Bronzeman*'s attempt to generate additional income among its readers, the deepening Depression all but negated these ameliorative efforts. As the magazine's circulation income declined, its operating costs became prohibitive. Notwithstanding the *Bronzeman*'s literary deficiencies, the magazine's investors spared no expense to ensure the excellence of its paper quality, print, and artwork.[23] Yet after chief investor Robert A. Cole lost a reported $30,000 by 1933,[24] Fireside Publications' Board of Directors decided the *Bronzeman* should meet an unfortunate, but financially expedient, demise.

Although the *Bronzeman* had flaws, this project's experimental nature should be stressed. Neither Robert A. Cole nor his MFSA associates had previous experience in the publishing field. Moreover, Caswell W. Crews and Henry Bacon, who served as the magazine's editor and managing editor, appear to have been as obscure as the talent featured in the periodical. Still, the *Bronzeman* ultimately reached both a national and international black audience.

Along with the Metropolitan Funeral System Association's direct involvement with Jack L. Cooper's "The All Negro Hour" and the ill-fated *Bronzeman* magazine, President Robert A. Cole, along with MFSA associate Horace G. Hall, participated in yet another high-profile Depression-era project. In February 1932, Cole purchased the Chicago American Giants of the Negro Baseball Leagues. Cole's subsequent involvement in black baseball, although significant in its own right, illuminated a nation-wide trend in African American communities during this period.

The Great Depression had an especially deleterious effect upon black communities throughout America. Black businessmen and their enter-prises were among the chief casualties of this economic downturn. Still, while black banks, manufacturing concerns, and retail outlets were closing across the United States, another community-based enterprise, seemingly unaffected by worsening economic conditions, rose to prominence. The "numbers racket" or "policy" rapidly eclipsed "legitimate" black business as the primary economic force in Depression-era black communities. Al-though there was relatively little, if any, stigma (among blacks) attached to being involved with "policy,"[25] "numbers bosses" nonetheless sought re-spectability by investing gambling profits in "legitimate" businesses. Black baseball was an enterprise that attracted considerable gambling profits.[26]

It appears the Negro Baseball Leagues would not have survived the Depression without the involvement of black gamblers. Despite the talent of Satchel Paige, Josh Gibson, and other black baseball stars, white major league teams, because of racism, probably would not have secured these players had the black leagues dissolved during the 1930s. Conse-quently, the survival of the Negro Baseball Leagues provided black players a continued opportunity to play organized baseball that ulti-mately led to their recruitment onto major league teams.

Gus Greenlee, the "numbers king" of Pittsburgh, was the most influen-tial black gambler turned baseball team owner. He organized the Pitts-burgh Crawfords in 1931. Josh Gibson, Satchel Paige, and "Cool Papa" Bell were among the stars Greenlee's "laundered" gambling profits attracted.[27] Alex Pompez, owner of the New York Cubans, Ed "Soldier Boy" Semler, owner of the Baltimore Elite Giants, Abe Manley, owner of the Newark Eagles, and Ed Bolden, owner of the Philadelphia Stars, were other prominent "underworld" figures who revived black baseball in their respective locales.[28]

While Robert A. Cole was reportedly not directly involved with "policy,"[29] his expertise in poker and blackjack permitted him to invest his winnings in a variety of projects, including the Metropolitan Funeral Parlors, the *Bronzeman,* and the Chicago American Giants. Cole, similar to his cohorts in other cities, viewed ownership of the American Giants as a means to enhance his respectability and prestige. While Cole's owner-ship of the American Giants can be seen as self-serving, it also appears he bought the team to ensure the survival of a Bronzeville institution.

Rube Foster, the Chicago American Giants' first owner, has been described by a black baseball historian as ". . . the most important influence in raising the game to respectability, both artistically, and financial."[30] Before his 1926 mental breakdown (caused by overwork) and his subsequent death in 1930, Foster had organized previously barnstorming black baseball teams into a Negro National League and had built the American Giants into the League's powerhouse.[31] Foster's health, the Chicago American Giants, and the Negro National League rapidly deteriorated between 1926 and 1930. When Robert A. Cole purchased the team from white florist William E. Trimble in early 1932, the American Giants were a sickly shadow of their former selves.[32]

Cole announced plans for the American Giants' rejuvenation shortly after purchasing the team. During a February 25, 1932, interview with the Chicago *Defender*, Cole asserted that his first priority was renovating Schorling Park, the Giants' home field located at 39th and Wentworth.[33] The American Giants purchased Schorling Park, the first home of the Chicago White Sox, after Charles Comiskey moved the White Sox to their current 35th Street location.[34] Schorling Park, named after Rube Foster's white business partner John Schorling, fell into disrepair during Rube Foster's prolonged illness. Among the scheduled improvements Cole planned to make were replacing the old bleachers and stands with new seating, installing modern dugouts and showers for the players, and constructing a press box.[35]

Besides renovating Schorling Park, subsequently renamed Cole Park, Robert A. Cole informed the *Defender* that he planned to rejuvenate the team itself. Noting that he instructed team manager Dave Malarcher to go after such stars as Satchel Paige, Cole further asserted: "Other owners get the best, so why can't we have the men we want? If my manager can't get them, I'll get down to work myself and see what Robert can do."[36]

Although Cole could not wrest Satchel Paige from Gus Greenlee's Pittsburgh Crawfords, the Giants' 1932 season was an unqualified suc-cess. The team, renamed Cole's American Giants, won the Southern League* pennant.[37]

---

*The Southern League replaced the then-moribund Negro National League.

The next year the powerful Gus Greenlee reorganized the Negro National Baseball League. This new circuit included the Crawfords, the American Giants, the Indianapolis ABCs, the Detroit Stars, the Homestead Grays, and the Columbus Blue Birds. The Homestead Grays and the Indianapolis ABCs, because of financial troubles, left at mid-season and were replaced by the Nashville Elite Giants and the Baltimore Black Sox.[38]

Cole's American Giants continued their winning ways in the reorganized Negro National League. They edged out Greenlee's Pittsburgh Crawfords for the league's first-half championship. Because of the Negro National League's incessant financial difficulties (even with the backing of black gamblers), the second half of the 1933 season was not completed. Under the structure of black baseball, the teams with the best records during the seasons's first and second halves played to determine the overall champion. Cole's American Giants, winners of the first half season pennant, claimed the league championship. Although the American Giants had a legitimate claim, Negro National League president Gus Greenlee ultimately declared his Crawfords were league champions for 1933.[39]

While financial instability and Greenlee's heavyhanded tactics marred the 1933 Negro National League season, it did have one exceptionally bright moment. A cooperative effort between (future enemies) Robert A. Cole and Gus Greenlee resulted in the inauguration of the annual East vs. West All-Star Game at Chicago's Comiskey Park.[40]

Cole, despite initial enthusiasm concerning the American Giants, sold his interest in the team to MFSA associate Horace G. Hall in 1935.[41] It appears that Cole's mounting financial difficulties with the Metropolitan Funeral Parlors, along with his mounting dislike for Gus Greenlee, prompted his decision to sell.

Horace G. Hall, the American Giants' new owner, had served as Cole's general manager and was an avid baseball fan.[42] His formation of the Negro American League in 1937 represented Hall's most noteworthy achievement as American Giants president. Besides the American Giants, the Negro American League included franchises in Kansas City, Birmingham, Memphis, and St. Louis.[43] Since most teams in the Negro National League were eastern-based; the Negro American League, comprised chiefly of midwestern and southern clubs, gave organized black baseball geographic balance.

Besides engaging in such high-profile independent endeavors as the

Bronzeman and the Chicago American Giants, Metropolitan Funeral System Association personnel actively worked with community organizations concerned with racial progress. The Wabash Avenue YMCA and the Chicago NAACP received especially notable support from the company.

The Wabash Avenue YMCA, located at 38th and Wabash, opened on June 15, 1913. Funds generated from within the black community, along with generous donations from white Chicagoans Julius Rosenwald and Cyrus McCormick, financed this facility's construction.[44] Allan Spear's 1967 study, *Black Chicago: The Making of a Negro Ghetto, 1890–1920,* asserted that increased black community pride, along with increased white racism, prompted the building of this black Chicago institution.[45] Regardless of the philosophical justification for its establishment, the Wabash Avenue YMCA provided much needed assistance to black Chicagoans. A boy's summer camp, a summer school affiliated with the Chicago Public Schools, meeting rooms for community organizations, monthly medical examinations for school children, and living facilities for transient males were among the services offered by this YMCA branch.[46]

The Great Depression adversely affected the Wabash Avenue YMCA. As early as 1928, this branch's executive secretary, George R. Arthur, warned Bronzeville's business and professional community that without its continued support the branch's services would be reduced.[47] Although black Chicago's most prominent businessmen, including Robert S. Abbott and Robert A. Cole, were members of the Wabash Avenue YMCA Board of Directors, these men (and their cohorts) had individual worries concerning the Depression. To compensate for the subsequent reduction of support from Bronzeville's elite, the Wabash Avenue YMCA began an accelerated membership drive aimed at Bronzeville's working class during the mid-1930s.

Robert A. Cole, along with five other prominent black Chicagoans, volunteered to coordinate the Wabash Avenue YMCA's 1935 membership drive.[48] Cole's exemplary efforts were later applauded.[49] Attorney James B. Cashin, another MFSA associate, acted as chairman of the 1938 membership campaign.[50] The Metropolitan Funeral System Associations's James D. Grantham, elected to the Wabash Avenue YMCA Board of Directors in January 1938, helped coordinate the 1939 membership drive.[51]

The National Association for the Advancement of Colored People (NAACP) was another racial uplift institution conspicuously supported by the Metropolitan Funeral System Association. The MFSA Board of

Directors, especially Robert A. Cole, strongly urged employees to become dues-paying NAACP members.[52] The NAACP rewarded Cole's efforts by featuring him on the cover of the January 1938 issue of *Crisis*.[53]

The Metropolitan Funeral System Association and Robert A. Cole's involvement with community improvement projects and organizations elicited a favorable response from Bronzeville residents. However, the company's initial involvement with community politics appeared far less successful.

In 1930, Oscar DePriest campaigned for reelection to the United States House of Representatives. DePriest, first elected in 1928, enjoyed immense popularity in Bronzeville because of his ardent espousal of racial justice. Among the challengers for DePriest's Illinois First Congressional District seat was Roscoe Conkling Simmons, a nephew of Booker T. Washington's third wife. Because Simmons had been politically aligned with the recently deceased Dan Jackson, MFSA supported him instead of Oscar DePriest. During the campaign, company agents sought to persuade policyholders to vote for Simmons.[54] Despite this support, DePriest convincingly defeated Simmons. Simmons's defeat, along with embarrassing (but unsubstantiated) allegations that company funds were illegally used to support Simmons, prompted the Metropolitan Funeral System Association to quickly abandon overt participation in the political arena.[55] Several individual employees, nonetheless, subsequently gained fame as politicians and public servants.[56]

Bronzeville politics, Jack L. Cooper's "The All Negro Hour," the Chicago American Giants, and the Wabash Avenue YMCA seem dissimilar on the surface. Yet in actuality they were part of the same process. All contributed to the adjustment of black southern migrants to permanent settlement in Chicago. All also solidified Robert A. Cole's reputation as a concerned citizen and undoubtedly helped boost MFSA profits.

The dramatic growth of Chicago's black population, beginning with the World War I "Great Migration," appeared linked to employment opportunities. Yet when these opportunities diminished, beginning in the 1920s, Bronzeville residents did not return to the South. A major reason they remained in Chicago was the existence of community-based institutions and activities. Besides such high-profile black Chicago institutions as the NAACP and the Urban League, a myriad of social and fraternal organizations existed in post–"Great Migration" Bronzeville.[57]

During the 1920s and 1930s, black Chicago social and cultural organizations were denied use of ballroom facilities in downtown hotels.[58]

Although there were approximately seventy-five public halls in Bronzeville that could accommodate at least 100 persons, most were in varying states of disrepair.[59] The lack of first-class recreational facilities in black Chicago partially motivated MFSA's 1940 construction of the Parkway Ballroom.

When the Parkway Ballroom opened during the summer of 1940, it represented an important racial achievement. While it was not the first black-sponsored attempt to bring recreational elegance to Bronzeville,[60] the Parkway Ballroom represented black economic self-determination at a time when whites were gaining increased control over black Chicago's retail and entertainment economy.

The Great Depression destroyed the historic black-controlled 35th and State Street commercial district.[61] Consequently, the hub of Bronzeville's economy (both retail and recreational) shifted to the white-controlled 47th and South Parkway (now King Drive) area. The construction of the Savoy Ballroom at 47th and South Parkway, by a consortium of white businessmen, exemplified this trend.

The Savoy Ballroom did provide black Chicagoans a variety of activities, including dances, boxing matches, roller skating, and big-band concerts. Still, the profits from these functions left black Chicago.[62] Moreover, many white-owned Bronzeville night spots had a "Jim Crow" seating policy during the 1930s and 1940s. Whites were seated near the stage and blacks sat in the rear.[63] The Parkway Ballroom provided black Chicagoans an elegant alternative to enriching absentee landlords or enduring racial insults.

Many considered the Parkway Ballroom, during its heyday, to be the best black-owned business of its type in the United States. Moreover, an informed source has asserted that during the 1940s and 1950s, the Parkway Ballroom was the finest ballroom in America (black or white) that was not affiliated with a hotel.[64] Besides providing first-class facilities to Bronzeville's social and cultural organizations, artists such as Duke Ellington and Count Basie regularly appeared at the Parkway.[65] With the decline of the white-owned Savoy Ballroom during the 1940s (partially caused by the Parkway Ballroom's growing popularity), the Parkway Ballroom became the undisputed hub of Bronzeville social activities.[66]

According to Clarence M. Markham, Jr., who founded *The Negro Traveler and Conventioneer* magazine in 1943, the Parkway Ballroom, during the 1940s and 1950s, was also a favorite of black visitors to Chicago. At a time when downtown Chicago stood "off-limits" to African

American travelers and conventioneers, the Parkway Ballroom represented a godsend to black visitors seeking an elegant place to relax and socialize.[67]

The Parkway Ballroom's initial success contributed to Metropolitan Mutual's 1948 decision to construct an adjacent facility known as the Parkway Dining Room. This restaurant, completed in 1949, provided company personnel and Bronzeville residents a first-class eating facility.[68] Noted for an extensive menu that included filet mignon,[69] the Parkway Dining Room attracted especially large crowds on Sundays and holidays.[70]

Another popular aspect of the Parkway Dining Room was its courteous waiter service.[71] Blacks in Chicago, similar to their brethren in other cities, were uncertain as to how they would be treated in restaurants. Black diners in white-owned restaurants frequently experienced slow service or outright verbal abuse. Unfortunately, the majority of black-owned eating establishments were "chicken shacks" or "rib joints." These facilities, while fine for a snack, were unsuitable for a formal dinner. The Parkway Ballroom, with its exquisitely dressed waiters, provided Bronzeville residents a means to enjoy the amenities associated with formal dining without having to risk insult.[72]

While the Parkway Ballroom and Dining Room were a boon to black Chicagoans, some white Chicagoans, too, applauded the existence of these facilities. Because the Parkway Ballroom Dining Room and Dining Room compared favorably to downtown establishments, some whites hoped that black Chicagoans would not be terribly concerned with desegregating Loop facilities.[73] Still, Bronzeville residents, similar to African Americans throughout the United States, caught the desegregation fever generated by the Supreme Court's monumental May 17, 1954, decision in *Brown vs. Board of Education of Topeka, Kansas.*

The arrival of de jure desegregation resulted in black access to facilities previously closed to them. It also resulted in the deterioration of institutions that sustained African Americans before their increased social mobility. Racial desegregation's effect upon the Parkway Ballroom and Dining Room offered a prime example of this phenomenon.

Downtown Chicago hotels, beginning in the mid-1950s, began to make their ballroom facilities available to Bronzeville social and cultural organizations. Although black organizations were often charged higher rental rates than similar white groups, it quickly became fashionable to conduct Bronzeville's social activities downtown.[74] Meanwhile, the Parkway Ballroom and Dining Room's popularity declined.

It appears that African Americans gradually abandoned the Parkway Ballroom and Dining Room partially because of the novelty involved with congregating downtown. Moreover, black Chicagoans, after gaining access to previously "off-limits" facilities, sought to continually extend the boundaries of their newfound social mobility. While some blacks characterized this phenomenon as progress, other lamented the resulting decline of Bronzeville institutions. Among African Americans, the debate continues as to whether the "gains" associated with racial desegregation compensated for the "losses."

The Metropolitan Funeral System Association, besides providing for Bronzeville residents' recreational needs, influenced the positive development of family life. Since the family unit represented black Chicago's primary social institution, the company's insurance and mortgage loan programs, which provided for the current and future needs of black Chicago families, were important contributions to community and family stability.

Before white-owned insurance companies renewed their interest in black consumers during the 1960s (see chapter 6), the black insurance industry, personified by the National Negro Insurance Association (NNIA), catered to the needs of black families. This organization, founded in 1921, informed African Americans of insurance's role as a provider of family economic stability.[75] During a period when white companies considered blacks "bad risks," African American insurance companies affiliated with the National Negro Insurance Association* offered their brethren the economic benefits associated with insurance coverage.

The Metropolitan Funeral System Association, besides belonging to the NNIA, was a member of the Chicago Negro Insurance Association* founded in 1936. This organization, aligned with the National Negro Insurance Association, sought to foster cooperation among black Chicago insurance firms.[76] Similar to the NNIA, the Chicago Negro Insurance Association informed Bronzeville residents of the benefits associated with owning insurance.[77] In addition, CNIA companies, unlike most Chicago banks, provided mortgage money to Bronzeville families seeking to become homeowners.[78]

---

*In 1954, the organization dropped the word "Negro" from its corporate name. It is currently called the National Insurance Association.

*In 1950, the Chicago Negro Insurance Association deleted the word "Negro" from its organizational title.

By the mid-1950s, the Chicago Metropolitan Mutual Assurance Company had become recognized as one of the (renamed) Chicago Insurance Association's most socially responsible members. Despite the company's extensive mortgage loan program and such high visibility projects as the Parkway Ballroom and Dining Room, it appeared CMMAC's most important contribution to black Chicago was its long-time promotion of community pride.

Besides the personal predilections and experiences of company founders Robert A. Cole and Fred W. Lewing, the teachings of Booker T. Washington motivated the Metropolitan Funeral System Association's commitment to community improvement. Washington's famous admonition, "cast your bucket where you are," influenced the company's initial decision to cater to the needs of Bronzeville's substantial working class.[79] Consequently, during CMMAC's early history, the company and its personnel (all of whom lived in Bronzeville) continually sought to make black Chicago a more desirable place to live. This fact remains undiminished despite black Chicagoans' subsequent focus on options outside of Bronzeville.

The Metropolitan Funeral System Association (later MMACC and CMMAC), in adherence to the maxim "good will begins at home," consistently sought to improve its employees' standard of living. During Robert A. Cole's presidency, company personnel received benefits that were the envy of other black Chicago workers. Employees, in return, gave Cole and the company their undivided loyalty. The subject of management-labor relations, especially within a historic African American business enterprise, merits a detailed examination.

V

THE CHICAGO METROPOLITAN "FAMILY," 1927–1957

During Chicago Metropolitan's formative years, employee solidarity, often described as the company "family,"[1] contributed mightily to its development as an African American community institution. Guided by the maxim "happy workers are productive workers," Robert A. Cole created an environment that, despite elements of paternalism, promoted internal harmony and profitability. Moreover, Cole, throughout his presidency, sought to provide policyholders with courteous and innovative service. Still, despite Cole's efforts, within a year of his death the company experienced severe internal dissension from which it never fully recovered.

Robert A. Cole, a naturally gregarious and generous man, relished his role as company patriarch.[2] Significantly, Cole's inclination toward paternalism, while reflective of personal traits, corresponded with the leadership style of other early black insurance company chief executives. As Walter B. Weare and Alexa B. Henderson noted in their respective studies of North Carolina Mutual and Atlanta Life, black insurance company presidents tended to be "approachable" individuals whose multifaceted interest in employees created a close-knit atmosphere.[3]

The evidence suggests that the special relationship between black insurance company patriarchs and their employees reflected these firms' unique place among African Americans. Unlike the majority of historic and contemporary black business enterprises which were (and are) tenuous single proprietorships,[4] black insurance companies were able to accumulate significant working capital. Although their assets paled in comparison to similar white institutions,[5] these companies represented the zenith of African American economic development. Consequently, the persons who managed and worked at these firms developed a special sense of pride and collective mission.

The occupational status of most early twentieth century blacks further stimulated the pride associated with working for a black insurance company. During this period the majority of African Americans were employed as unskilled or semi-skilled laborers. Moreover, many of these positions, such as menial industrial labor (under white supervision) and personal service jobs, were markedly reminiscent of the duties performed by their slave forebears. Granted, the Metropolitan Funeral System Association, and similar black companies, employed a relatively small number of African Americans in clerical, sales, and managerial positions. Still, the existence of these black-created jobs, however limited, appears historically significant.

While working for a black insurance company provided employees with psychic and occupational rewards, Robert A. Cole also sought to enhance the lifestyle of his employees. Cole's benevolence toward workers, while partially prompted by generosity, demonstrated his gratitude for employee loyalty during the company's tenuous first decade.

Robert A. Cole's initial years as president of the Metropolitan Funeral System Association were characterized by a flurry of personal activity. Cole, who seemed to have been a natural promoter, spent more time making deals in the streets than he spent at MFSA headquarters.[6] Fred W. Lewing's indomitable presence as general manager allowed Cole the freedom to pursue other interests.[7]

Robert A. Cole's substantial gambling winnings enabled him to pursue a variety of financial ventures. Still, Cole, like most gamblers, did experience losing streaks. One particularly untimely losing streak occurred in 1931. This run of bad luck coincided with worsening economic conditions associated with the Great Depression.

As black Chicagoans' income decreased, thousands allowed their MFSA policies to lapse.[8] Considering that the company's 1930 move to 418 E. 47th Street represented a substantial investment, MFSA policyholders' growing lapse rate caused concern within the company. Since 1927, Cole periodically used his own money to buttress MFSA's financial stability. Yet decreased 1931 gambling revenues, along with decreased MFSA income from policyholders premium payments, forced Cole to borrow money for such basic company expenses as payroll and utility costs.[9]

As Cole increased his indebtedness to Jim Nash, owner of the Palm Tavern, a popular 47th Street establishment, it soon appeared that either

Jim Nash would ultimately control the company or MFSA would fold. Just when it appeared that Cole's legendary good luck had run out, General Manager Fred W. Lewing stepped forward with a bold proposal.[10]

Lewing calculated that if the company's weekly premium income could be increased from $5,000 to $7,500 during an intensive two-week campaign, Cole could cease borrowing to meet essential expenses.[11] Considering that Lewing came to this conclusion while policy lapses were increasing, his hopes appeared unrealistic. Still, against enormous odds, Lewing and his agency force somehow accomplished this task.[12] Although Cole's luck changed for the better in late 1931, he apparently never forgot how company agents had rallied to his support. Moreover, he spent the rest of his life expressing his gratitude.

Besides the herculean effort by MFSA agents during the crisis of 1931, the company's early legal problems also contributed to the development of the Chicago Metropolitan "family." The Alfred Nelson affair was especially significant.

Alfred Nelson, the prominent agent turned company critic, considered himself a champion of policyholders' rights. For instance, he believed the weekly salaries given Cole, Lewing, and Rayner ($250, $100, and $100) at the December 23, 1929, general meeting were unjustified. Nelson asserted that this money should be used to increase policyholder benefits.[13] He also criticized the Cole administration's policy of accumulating surplus reserves. Once again, Nelson argued that this money should be returned to policyholders in the form of increased benefits.[14]

Another Nelson indictment of the Cole administration was its failure to post sufficient bond with the Illinois Department of Insurance. The Metropolitan Policyholders Protective Association prominently featured this fact in its 1932 suit against MFSA.[15] While Nelson hoped to use this situation to prove the Cole administration's malfeasance, the evidence suggested otherwise.

When Robert A. Cole reorganized MFSA in late 1927, the State of Illinois loosely regulated burial associations. It took only an $800 bond filed with the Cook County Treasurer to begin operations.[16] By 1929, as burial associations began to proliferate in Illinois, the Illinois Department of Insurance began to take a more active role in regulating these entities. The department subsequently ruled that Illinois-domiciled burial associations must post a $5,000 bond with its office.[17] MFSA duly complied with this new measure.[18]

On July 3, 1931, the Illinois Department of Insurance again revised regulations concerning burial insurance associations. The new guidelines stated:

> ... all such societies having more than 10,000 members shall deposit with the said Department (Illinois Department of Insurance) the sum of ten thousand dollars and an additional one thousand dollars for each 1,000 members in excess of 10,000.[19]

When the Illinois Department of Insurance conducted its June 10, 1932, examination of MFSA, it found the company had not complied with the new provisions.[20] Since MFSA then had a reported 39,000 policyholders, the company needed to deposit an additional $34,000 with the department.

Despite this major oversight, the June 10, 1932, examination of the company concluded:

> It is noted by your examiners that the officers of this association are very anxious and willing to conduct the business in strict conformity with the requirements of the Insurance Department and we wish to express our appreciation for the consideration and cooperation shown us by the officers and employees throughout the conduct of this examination.[21]

Still, Alfred Nelson, in a conscious attempt to defame the Cole administration, widely publicized MFSA's failure to post sufficient bond with the state.[22]

When Alfred Nelson and his Metropolitan Policyholders Protective Association filed their 1932 suit against MFSA, persons associated with the company were forced to take sides in the dispute. Although Nelson had a number of supporters, the Metropolitan Policyholders Protective Association represented a distinct minority among MFSA personnel and policyholders. Consequently, the majority overwhelmingly rejected Nelson's 1934 bid for board membership.[23] This demonstration of support for the Cole administration resulted in Nelson and his followers leaving MFSA and further predisposed Cole toward assuming the role of beneficent patriarch.

Alfred Nelson's efforts were ironic in that they resulted in his, rather than the Cole administration's, humiliation. Nelson failed because, despite his allegations, the majority of MFSA policyholders were pleased with the company. Besides the Metropolitan Funeral System Association's economical burial policies, policyholders truly appreciated the efforts of Rev. Mansfield Edward Bryant Peck, the company's social service director. Peck made a point of visiting and assisting the families of deceased policyholders.[24] His sensitivity made policyholders feel like part of a family, rather than part of an impersonal business entity. President Robert A. Cole, moreover, sought to enhance family-like relations between MFSA and its policyholders by sponsoring summer picnics where both company personnel and policyholders were invited.[25]

Besides Nelson's lack of success with MFSA policyholders, he had even worse results in attempting to recruit company employees to his cause. Although the personalities of President Robert A. Cole and General Manager Fred W. Lewing elicited the respect and admiration of most company personnel, there was another reason for their rejection of Nelson's movement. Shortly after Robert A. Cole reorganized MFSA, Fred W. Lewing informed employees that subsequent managerial and administrative positions would be filled with existing personnel.[26] Lewing's pledge resulted in the development of a solid core of highly motivated and loyal people. Considering the dearth of managerial and administrative positions available to African Americans during this period,[27] Nelson's actions, which may be viewed as being based upon egotism rather than altruism,[28] were judged as detrimental to employee interests and subsequently rejected.*

After surviving a myriad of threats to its existence, the Cole administration decided to construct a new home office to celebrate MFSA's durability and vitality. The resulting structure, completed in 1940, also provided Cole a means to repay policyholders and personnel for their loyalty during difficult times. While Alfred Nelson probably would have considered the new home office a frivolous expenditure, the vast majority of persons affiliated with the company welcomed the new edifice.

Metropolitan Funeral System Association personnel relocated company operations in a unique fashion when the new home office stood ready for occupancy in August 1940. Company agents marched from 418 E. 47th Street (the company's old headquarters) to 4455 South Parkway carrying MFSA records. During the agents' two-block march down one of Bronzeville's busiest streets, onlookers viewed the proceedings approvingly; some even cheered.[29]

---

*When the company became a legal reserve firm in 1946, outside managerial staff had to be brought in because existing personnel lacked sufficient expertise in marketing ordinary life insurance.

A week-long grand opening celebration, held from September 7 to 13, continued the excitement generated by the agents' dramatic march. The modernity of the company's new headquarters and the elegance of the adjacent Parkway Ballroom enthralled policyholders and other visitors.[30] Moreover, to assist persons in appreciating what the company called "A Monument to Bronze America," MFSA distributed a souvenir book which, among other things, advised:

> When you enter these exquisite buildings, look carefully around you. Every detail of efficiency and comfort has been provided. A pleasant air of cheerful modernity permeates you and those who serve you. . . . These walls are made for your contentment. Let their gracious colors talk to you. Here are the joys that delight the senses. All the wisdom of architecture waits you here. Revel in them, enjoy them. They are yours.[31]

Although the above description seemed overdone, most observers considered the opening of MFSA's new home as an important event. The new MFSA home office was Chicago's first large-scale black-controlled construction project since the heyday of the old 35th and State Street business district.* Yet, while MFSA officials were concerned with enhancing the larger community, the new home office's primary purpose was to provide personnel and policyholders a luxurious place to work, transact business, and relax.†

Among the on-site benefits subsequently made available to employees were bowling alleys, a recreation room equipped with pool and billiard tables, a sauna, and a masseur.[32] Continuous piped-in music from Muzak represented another feature of MFSA's new headquarters.[33]

---

*Among the prominent black-financed buildings constructed in the 35th and State Street district were: the Jordan Building, financed by African American songwriter Joseph J. Jordan, located at 3529–49 S. State Street (1916–1917); the Overton Hygienic Company / Douglass National Bank Building, financed by black businessman Anthony Overton, located at 3619-27 S. State Street (1922–1923); and the Binga Arcade, a five-story structure, financed by African American businessman and realtor Jesse Binga, located on the northeast corner of 35th and State Street (1928–1929). See "Black Metropolis Historic District," Preliminary Summary of Information, submitted to the Commission on Chicago Historical and Architectural Landmarks, March 7, 1984.

†Cole's emphasis on a luxurious new home office later drew the ire of the Illinois Department of Insurance. The department, in a March 28, 1941, letter to MFSA, admonished Cole for spending more on the project than originally agreed. While Cole's response is not extant, evidence suggests that Cole probably justified the additional expense by noting the significant increase in company premium income generated from Bronzeville's favorable response to the new home office (see chapter 1, table 1–4).

Inside cover of the 1930 company publication, *A Place in the Sun.* Courtesy of Robert A. Cole, Jr.

Fred W. Lewing. Circa 1930s. Courtesy of Robert A. Cole, Jr.

Ahmad A. Rayner. Circa 1930s.
Courtesy of Robert A. Cole, Jr.

Robert A. Cole. Circa 1930s. Courtesy of Robert A. Cole, Jr.

Horace G. Hall, company official who served as general manager of the Chicago American Giants (under Cole) and later owned the team. Circa 1930s. Courtesy of Robert A. Cole, Jr.

Agency Department superintendents, 1930. Alfred Nelson, who became an outspoken company critic, is seated at the far left. Courtesy of Robert A. Cole, Jr.

Edith Lautier, first supervisor of the
company's Clerical Department. Circa
1930s. Courtesy of Robert A. Cole, Jr.

Scene from home office operations at 418 E. 47th Street. Circa 1930s.
Courtesy of Robert A. Cole, Jr.

Scene from the 1939 East-West Negro Leagues All-Star Game at Chicago's Comiskey Park. Robert A. Cole watches heavyweight boxing champion Joe Louis throw the first pitch. Courtesy of Robert A. Cole, Jr.

Agency Department meeting, 1940. Courtesy of the Chicago Metropolitan Assurance Company.

Company employees standing outside the recently completed new home
office at 4455 South Parkway (now Dr. Martin Luther King, Jr. Drive),
1940. Courtesy of the Chicago Metropolitan Assurance Company.

Robert A. Cole posing with First Lady Eleanor Roosevelt after his 1942
Chicago speech urging greater business support of the war effort.
Courtesy of Robert A. Cole, Jr.

Metropolitan Mutual Assurance Company of Chicago, East St. Louis, Illinois, Office, 1507 East Broadway. Circa 1951. Courtesy of the Chicago Metropolitan Assurance Company.

Scene from the company's twenty-fifth anniversary celebration, December 29, 1952. Standing left to right are: Robert A. Cole; his daughter, Roberta; his wife, Mary F. Cole; and his son, Robert A. Cole, Jr. Courtesy of Robert A. Cole, Jr.

The company's home office complex, the northeast corner of 45th and South Parkway. Circa 1950s. Courtesy of the Metropolitan Assurance Company.

Last photograph of Robert A. Cole, taken thirteen days before his July 27, 1956, death. Courtesy of the Chicago Metropolitan Assurance Company.

The January 20, 1958, commemorative service honoring Robert A. Cole and Fred W. Lewing in the company's home office lobby. From left to right are: James D. Grantham, Horace G. Hall, Thomas P. Harris, Reverend Richard Keller, George S. Harris (obscured), and Melvin McNairy. Courtesy of the Chicago Metropolitan Assurance Company.

Scene from "Secretaries Day," 1959. Courtesy of the Chicago Metropolitan Assurance Company.

Board of Directors meeting, 1965. From left to right are: Dr. Edward Beasley, Horace G. Hall, George S. Harris, Thomas P. Harris, James D. Grantham, James W. Tyler, and Lorenzo Jones. Courtesy of the Chicago Metropolitan Assurance Company.

Scene from the company's fortieth anniversary celebration, 1967. Standing left to right are: Melvin McNairy, Lorenzo Jones, James W. Tyler, Emma Hodge (one of the pioneers in the Clerical Department), James D. Grantham, George S. Harris, Thomas P. Harris, Horace G. Hall, and Anderson M. Schweich. Courtesy of the Chicago Metropolitan Assurance Company.

Bowen M. Heffner. Circa 1960s. Courtesy of the Chicago Metropolitan
Assurance Company.

Home Office. Circa 1969. Courtesy of the Chicago Metropolitan Assurance
Company.

Scene from company Christmas party, December 1970. Courtesy of the Chicago Metropolitan Assurance Company.

Anderson M. Schweich. Circa 1970s. Courtesy of the Chicago Metropolitan Assurance Company.

Retirement party celebrating Melvin McNairy's forty-five years with the company, 1972. From left to right are: Melvin McNairy, George S. Harris, and Anderson M. Schweich. Courtesy of the Chicago Metropolitan Assurance Company.

Metropolitan Funeral Parlors. Circa 1970s. Courtesy of the Chicago *Defender.*

Lee L. Bailey, Josephine King, and Rumor L. Oden. Circa 1980s.
Courtesy of the Chicago Metropolitan Assurance Company.

Jesse L. Moman. Circa 1980s.
Courtesy of the Chicago
Metropolitan Assurance
Company.

Chicago Metropolitan's last officers before its 1990 purchase by Atlanta Life. Circa 1990. Sitting from left to right are: Weathers Y. Sykes, Senior Vice-President/Operations; Henry P. Hervey, Vice President/Investments; Josephine King, Senior Vice-President/Administration; Anderson M. Schweich, President/Chief Executive Officer; Clinton E. Ward, Vice-President/Controller. Standing from left to right are: Herbert W. Cooley, Assistant Vice-President/Agency Department; William Hargis, Assistant Vice-President/Agency Department; Hollis L. Green, Executive Vice-President/General Counsel; and John Fitzpatrick, Vice-President/Agency Director. Courtesy of the Chicago Metropolitan Assurance Company.

The Home Office after its renovation. Circa 1980s. Courtesy of the Chicago Metropolitan Assurance Company.

Josephine King. Circa 1990s. King is Chicago Metropolitan's current (and last) Chief Executive Officer. As a result of the company's purchase by Atlanta Life, the building at 4455 S. King Drive is scheduled to close sometime in 1996. Courtesy of the Chicago Metropolitan Assurance Company.

Policyholders, too, received special treatment in the new home office. The company furnished the cashier's section of the facility with plush couches for policyholders' comfort.[34] Also, if more than four policyholders were waiting in a line to pay their premiums, Robert A. Cole would often direct clerical workers to serve as temporary cashiers.[35]

Besides the plush office facilities provided personnel and policyholders, the company "family" extensively used the Parkway Ballroom and Dining Room. Although community organizations frequently rented out the Parkway Ballroom, employees regularly used it for after-work socializing. Annual meetings and the yearly Christmas party were among the structured company events held in the Parkway Ballroom. Company personnel and their friends especially anticipated the Christmas party because Cole provided free food, beverages, and entertainment.[36]

When the Parkway Dining Room opened in 1949, it provided good food, at economical cost, to both company personnel and the larger community. A liberal meal-ticket program allowed employees to purchase $10 worth of food tickets for $5.[37] Moreover, employees lucky (or astute) enough to be in the Parkway Dining Room when Robert A. Cole appeared for a meal were generally able to eat free at Cole's request.[38]

While Robert A. Cole provided all personnel with pleasant working conditions and a myriad of perquisites, agents also enjoyed considerable flexibility in servicing their debits. Agents were not under a mandatory 40-hour work week. If an agent spent 20, 30, 40, or 50 hours a week to service a debit, the company approved. MFSA (and its later derivatives) expected agents to "get the job done," rather than conform to an arbitrary time system.[39]

Although Agency Department supervisors gave their exclusively male workforce considerable latitude, MFSA closely supervised its primarily female home office clerical staff. The company's close surveillance of female personnel appeared based upon Robert A. Cole's paternalistic predilections concerning the role of women. Cole, similar to fathers who believe their sons need less supervision than their daughters, applied the same double standard to the "sons" and "daughters" of the company. While such paternalism can be stifling to the women involved, male proponents of this sentiment appear guilty of misguided chivalry rather than malevolence.

During the 1940s and 1950s, Rosalee Wood, the company's Clerical Department supervisor, coordinated the supervision of female personnel. Wood, unlike her assertive predecessor, Edith Lautier, assumed a less threatening posture toward the company's male hierarchy and complied with its wishes.

While company female personnel were subject to gender-specific supervision, they also received gender-specific benefits. For instance, a prominent Bronzeville modeling agency regularly provided female employees with free instruction in good grooming, speech, and manners.[40] Although these classes improved female employees' confidence, they were apparently meant to produce more effective and attractive secretaries, rather than prospective executives.

In our current era of more equitable gender relations, Robert A. Cole's treatment of female personnel seems patronizing. Still, despite the "Little Miss" designation he gave individual clerical workers,[41] in the context of its time black women at MFSA (and its later derivatives) were treated far better than their sisters at white companies. While Robert A. Cole apparently did not encourage women (other than his wife) to seek executive status, one credible female informant has asserted that during the 1940s and 1950s the majority of women were so socialized in their prescribed roles that they seldom considered climbing the corporate ladder.[42]

Whereas male and female workers were regarded differently by the patriarchal Robert A. Cole, all MFSA personnel were generally treated well in the larger community. Merchants, especially, accorded company employees considerable courtesy. A primary reason for MFSA employees' special status in black Chicago was the company's historic commitment to pay people on time.[43] Cole, as the crisis of 1931 indicated, willingly went into debt to ensure that his employees were paid.

MFSA's regular payment policy resulted in employees obtaining easy credit from community merchants.[44] Since company personnel were able to readily obtain such consumer items as automobiles and fashionable suits and dresses, MFSA (and later, CMMAC) employees soon became recognized as prosperous individuals. These consumer items, along with the company's plush home office and adjacent recreational facilities, helped to promote a dynamic image of company personnel in the eyes of other black Chicagoans.[45]

While company employees had access to a variety of special amenities, these did not supplant basic financial benefits. The wages of both agents and clerical personnel were competitive with other companies. The Metropolitan Mutual Assurance Company of Chicago also instituted a generous company-paid pension plan in 1952.[46] Considering that company employees received numerous perquisites, coupled with a sound salary and pension structure, it is not surprising that during Robert A. Cole's presidency jobs at CMMAC were at a premium. Nor is it surprising, given the generous benefits and Cole's paternalism, that union representation was not an issue.

Robert A. Cole was an anti-union employer.[47] While such a stance may evoke an unfavorable image, Cole's resistance to unions did not elicit the ire of personnel. To the contrary, the majority of employees during Cole's administration agreed that unions were unnecessary at Chicago Met.[48] Several reasons were cited for this situation.

First, Robert A. Cole, as a result of the 1931 premium income crisis, realized that his success as company president and employee performance were intimately related. Consequently, he felt compelled to serve his own best interest by catering to the needs of MFSA employees. While the maxim "happy workers are productive workers" appears amusingly quaint, Cole made this simple truism the cornerstone of his relationship with personnel.[49]

Besides Cole's concerted effort to provide employees with a myriad of benefits, his accessibility to personnel mitigated the need for a union at MFSA (and CMMAC). He maintained an "open door" policy to any employee with a complaint.[50] Cole's "down-to-earth" gregariousness, moreover, often had a tranquilizing effect on potentially disruptive situations.[51]

Another important reason for the absence of union activity during Cole's presidency was the company's policy of promoting from within. Although female employees' mobility appeared limited, ambitious male personnel had a concrete opportunity for advancement. Male employees, therefore, tended to focus upon becoming managers rather than criticizing them.[52]

Both employees and policyholders deeply mourned Robert A. Cole's death on July 27, 1956. Thomas P. Harris, Cole's successor, appeared eminently qualified to assume the company's leadership. Yet his personality prevented him from assuming Cole's role as gregarious company patriarch. Unlike the spontaneous Cole, Harris was a quiet, analytical attorney.[53] Moreover, Harris, upon assuming the presidency, had to address growing financial problems associated with Cole's generosity.

The Illinois Department of Insurance's March 15, 1957, examination of the Chicago Metropolitan Mutual Assurance Company reported substantial operating losses in 1955 and 1956.[54] Although the company's

TABLE 5–1
Home Office Income/Expenses,
Chicago Metropolitan Mutual Assurance Company,
1947–1956

	Income	Expenses	Net Loss
1947	$26,086	$36,140	$10,054
1948	24,601	29,581	4,980
1949	20,635	45,744	25,109
1950	44,789	62,443	17,655
1951	43,145	73,466	30,321
1952	40,813	76,725	35,912
1953	45,708	76,286	30,577
1954	51,584	101,902	50,318
1955	38,404	110,173	71,769
1956	42,000	96,323	54,323
Total	$377,765	$708,783	$331,018

Source: Illinois Department of Insurance Examinations of MMACC (later CMMAC), March 1, 1950, p. 21; October 30, 1953, p. 20; March 15, 1957, p. 30.

initial expansion into Indiana and Missouri had proceeded smoothly, other corporate projects, specifically the Parkway Ballroom and Dining Room, were losing money (see table 5–1).

The Parkway Amusement Corporation (PAC), a Chicago Metropolitan subsidiary, managed the Parkway Ballroom and Dining Room. The PAC was a "paper" corporation. While it ostensibly supplied the Parkway Ballroom with liquor and the Parkway Dining Room with food, Chicago Metropolitan actually financed these facilities' operating expenses.[55]

The Parkway Ballroom and Dining Room, despite their popularity, were comparatively poor income generators. The ballroom, especially, suffered deficits because the rent received from community organizations using the facility did not fully cover maintenance and utility costs. Significantly, Robert A. Cole apparently never expressed serious concern about the Parkway Ballroom and Dining Room's financial condition. In his view, these facilities provided public relations benefits of considerable value. Cole, moreover, through the Parkway Amusement Corporation, secured food and liquor (at wholesale cost) for company personnel as well as for the Parkway Ballroom and Dining Room.[56] Yet, to the exacting Thomas P. Harris, these and other expenses seemed excessive.[57]

While Thomas P. Harris's decision to trim fat from the Parkway Amusement Corporation represented a sound business maneuver, his simultaneous attempt to cut Agency Department expenses proved disastrous. Harris's measures precipitated an agent strike. The animosity created by this work stoppage greatly strained the company "family."

The Agency Department, during the halcyon days of the Cole administration, epitomized the "happy workers are productive workers" maxim. For instance, between the years 1947 and 1956, after the company's conversion from a burial association to a legal reserve company, the amount of industrial insurance in force grew from $29,358,445 to $87,874,822. Ordinary insurance in force increased from $2,600 to $5,969,888.[58] Still, Thomas P. Harris, during his assessment of company operations after Cole's death, decided that changes were needed within the Agency Department.

The luxury of hindsight indicates that Thomas P. Harris's 1956 decision to decrease the weekly commission of Chicago agents from 20 to 15 percent represented a grave miscalculation. By December 31, 1956, 161 (53 percent) of the company's 302 industrial debits were in the Chicago area. These 161 Chicago debits produced a weekly premium income of $61,424.07 or nearly 81 percent of the company's total industrial weekly debit of $75,996.59.[59] It appeared (on paper) that reducing Chicago agents' collection commission would save the company considerable money. While such a stance theoretically made sense, Chicago agents, grown used to Cole's generosity, resented Harris's decision. The company's decision not to implement a similar collection commission decrease among agents outside of Chicago made Bronzeville agents even angrier.[60] The Chicago Met board apparently believed that special agent incentives would stimulate the development of the downstate Illinois, Indiana, and Missouri territories.

Before Chicago-based agents actually went on strike during the summer of 1957, they attempted to negotiate with the company's leadership.[61] In times past, agents made a point of discussing their grievances with Robert A. Cole. Since Cole appeared predisposed to give agents a fair hearing, relations between agents and the company hierarchy were always cordial. However Harris, unlike Cole, believed he did not owe agents special consideration. Thus, agents who may have been "spoiled" by Cole's magnanimity would not accept Harris's apparent intransigence. Beginning in June 1957, Chicago agents began manning picket lines, rather than servicing their debits.

The Chicago Metropolitan Mutual Assurance Company experienced extreme trauma during the summer of 1957. The company, between

June and August, suffered in the areas of internal relations, relations between itself and policyholders, and its image in Bronzeville. Moreover, some believe Chicago Metropolitan never fully recovered from the negative repercussions of the 1957 agent strike.[62]

Perhaps the most significant aspect of the 1957 agent strike was its adverse effect on company morale. Company administrators and agents, who previously shared after-work cocktails in the Parkway Ballroom and games of pool in the basement recreation room, suddenly viewed each other as adversaries. Those few agents who refused to go on strike drew the wrath of their colleagues. One non-striking agent actually needed a police escort to service his debit.[63]

While the 1957 agent strike produced overt hostility between company management and agents, it also had a negative effect upon policyholders. During the strike, agents refused to collect premiums from policyholders. Consequently, policyholders were caught in a dilemma. Specifically, they were forced to ask themselves: "If we follow agents' instructions and do not pay our premiums, are we risking cancellation of our coverage?" Many policyholders grappled with this difficult situation throughout the strike. An unknown but significant number of policyholders solved the dilemma by leaving the company in disgust.[64]

Besides company policyholders, the 1957 agent strike shocked and confused the larger Bronzeville community. For decades the Chicago Metropolitan "family" had been a positive demonstration of collective economic development. Consequently, the 1957 agent strike jolted black Chicagoans, especially those who remembered company agents' triumphant 1940 march.

Despite the strike's adverse effect on Chicago Metropolitan's rapport with policyholders and the larger community, company management and agents were intransigent during the first weeks of the strike. As the work stoppage progressed, both sides became increasingly convinced that the "other side" intended to destroy them.[65]

This labor conflict's turning point occurred in early August when company electricians and air-conditioning technicians joined the agents.[66] On August 5, 1957, they shut off the home office's electricity and air-conditioning. This demonstration of labor solidarity stunned the company's Board of Directors. The board, after giving home office clerical personnel the rest of the day off, faced a tough decision. That evening, the Parkway Ballroom, now without air-conditioning, had been rented to hold an important community affair. The board, realizing that cancellation of this event would have been a major embarrassment, quickly agreed to recognize the legitimacy of the agents' grievances.[67]

Several persons have contended that the agent strike of 1957 would not have occurred had Robert A. Cole been alive.[68] While this appears to be a credible assumption, the problems faced by the company after Cole's death were inevitable. Consequently, after Cole died a serious reassessment of company operations would have been in order.

Robert A. Cole possessed considerable power during his twenty-nine year presidency of Chicago Metropolitan. Although he actively sought the advice of Fred W. Lewing, Horace G. Hall, James D. Grantham, and Thomas P. Harris, Cole apparently made the final decisions concerning company policy. The operation of the Parkway Ballroom and Dining Room during Cole's presidency offered a prime example of his overriding influence.

Although the evidence indicates that these two facilities were not profitable, Cole justified their existence by their entertainment and public relations value. Despite the fact that these facilities lost more than $300,000 between 1947 and 1956 (see table 5–1), Cole's overwhelming support of the Parkway Ballroom and Dining Room ensured their unmodified continuance.

When the scholarly Thomas P. Harris took control, he gave more attention to the company's balance sheet. While his move toward greater efficiency appeared justified, hindsight indicates that he should have undertaken this project more gradually. Chicago Metropolitan employees had gained a generous wage scale and numerous benefits over several years. Consequently, Harris's immediate attempt to cut agents' wages had a jolting effect that quickly led to outright hostility.

While some of Thomas P. Harris's initial difficulties seemed self-inflicted, his greatest early misfortune was succeeding the immensely popular Robert A. Cole. Cole, a proverbial "hard act to follow," had indelibly stamped his mark on the company's early history. While Harris was a brilliant lawyer and accomplished orator, he lacked the charisma of his predecessor. Moreover, in attempting to overturn a popular tradition that ran deeper than wages and benefits, it seemed predictable that Harris would encounter a dedicated opposition.

Unquestionably, the most unfortunate aspect of the pivotal 1957 agent strike was its adverse effect upon intracompany relations. The two-month work stoppage generated ill feelings that followed years of internal tranquility. Furthermore, this serious breach in company unity occurred at a time when the advent of racial desegregation posed a tremendous challenge to African American companies.

Chicago Metropolitan faced integration's challenge in a state of turmoil. Whereas the recently ended agent strike had been successfully settled, the company "family" remained far from happy. The selection of the hard-nosed Lorenzo D. Jones as the new agency director in September 1957 fueled lingering animosity. Still, despite Jones's and Thomas P. Harris's unpopularity among certain employees, these two men would subsequently use their considerable experience and ability to lead Chicago Metropolitan into an uncertain future.

VI

CHICAGO METROPOLITAN, 1958–1985

> If segregation were eliminated, the social justification for the existence of Negro business would vanish and the Negro would have to compete with other businessmen. Undoubtedly, many Negro business enterprises would disappear, along with the sentimental justification which helps support them.[1]

Chicago Metropolitan's history from 1958 to 1985 represented a struggle to survive in a changed world. Unfortunately for Chicago Met and other black insurers, racial integration proved to be a "one-way street." While previously discriminatory white insurance companies made considerable inroads among black consumers, Chicago Metropolitan and other black firms could not similarly attract white customers. Thus, in lieu of becoming an interracial company, Chicago Met solidified its historic preoccupation with black community development. Yet in the face of increased white competition the company never regained its earlier prominence.

In the wake of the 1957 agent strike, Chicago Metropolitan slowly recouped the momentum established by the Cole administration (see table 6–1). President Thomas P. Harris's and Agency Director Lorenzo D. Jones's more respectful attitude toward personnel, especially agents, helped this process. Both men, like the deceased Cole, began to fully realize that employee performance determined the company's success. Consequently, the period immediately following the strike witnessed an attempt to reinstate a family atmosphere within the company.

Thomas P. Harris, speaking at the January 20, 1958, annual meeting, attempted to rekindle the company unity damaged during the strike. He asserted that Chicago Met management and labor, at post-strike, were preparing to enter a new era of understanding and cooperation.[2]

TABLE 6–1
Weekly Premium Income,
Chicago Metropolitan Mutual Assurance Company,
1957–1959

	1957	1958	1959
Chicago	$54,713	$56,291	$60,533
Downstate	7,069	6,678	7,013
Indiana	3,984	3,421	3,862
Missouri	1,943	1,551	1,448
Ohio	—	724	480
Total	$67,709	$68,665	$73,336

Source: Minutes, Annual Meetings, CMMAC, January 20, 1958, January 19, 1959, January 18, 1960.

Harris continued his theme of internal reconciliation at the January 19, 1959, annual meeting. He urged personnel to recall the spirit of the company's founders, especially their "one-mindedness."[3]

Besides Harris's conciliatory statements, he, along with Agency Director Lorenzo D. Jones, sought to provide agents with benefits above and beyond those called for in the union settlement. In February 1958, the CMMAC Board of Directors passed a resolution that provided performance bonuses for agents.[4] In April 1959, Lorenzo D. Jones promoted the establishment of an August Jubilee "Homecoming Picnic." This recommendation, subsequently ratified by the Chicago Met board, sought to further improve intracompany relations, as well as to publicly recognize deserving agents.[5]

Chicago Metropolitan's post-strike attempt to regain its historic "family" atmosphere appeared to be based on more than sentimentality. Growing racial desegregation in Chicago meant that CMMAC employees, along with other Bronzeville residents, had expanded employment opportunities.[6] Black insurance agents, especially, had become sought-after commodities.[7]

For several decades, most mainstream insurance companies had either ignored black consumers or charged them excessive premium rates.[8] Still, Prudential, New York Life, and other large companies began to actively seek black clients as the African American standard of living began to rise during the late 1950s.[9] This development posed two distinct challenges to CMMAC and other black insurance companies. First, many black consumers, because they had been previously denied equitable coverage with industry giants, viewed prospective policies with mainstream companies as status symbols.[10] Second, large insurance companies decided to recruit black agents from black companies to service the African American consumer market. Thus mainstream giants, with promises of financial reward, were able to secure many trained black insurance agents.[11]

Considering the serious threat of growing white competition, CMMAC's reaffirmation of company solidarity was not surprising. In addition the company's leadership, hoping to better compete in an increasingly crowded marketplace, sought to raise agents' professional standards. Lorenzo D. Jones, shortly after becoming agency director in September 1957, proposed far-reaching reforms in the Agency Department.[12] Chief among Jones's recommendations was that CMMAC's Agency Department should be run according to guidelines established by the Life Insurance Agency Management Association (LIAMA).[13] To meet this goal, Jones purchased LIAMA instructional materials which were distributed to all agency personnel. He subsequently appointed Cleland Brewer, formerly with the black-owned Mammoth Life Insurance Company, to serve as a traveling "troubleshooter." Brewer's primary duty was to ensure that Jones's reforms were carried out in outlying districts.[14]

While white insurance companies' business in the African American community increased during the late 1950s and early 1960s, black insurance companies were not able to register similar gains among white consumers. Significantly, black companies put considerable effort into their quest to reach potential white clients. For instance, Chicago Metropolitan's Board of Directors passed a November 22, 1961, resolution that stated: ". . . it would be a future policy of the company to employ competent persons both in Agency and Office Administration without regard to race, creed, or color."[15] The Chicago Metropolitan Mutual Assurance Company subsequently interviewed several European Americans for positions in the company's Agency Department.[16] This attempt at racial desegregation, however, proved fruitless. While some black agents with black companies eagerly defected to white-owned companies, white insurance agents were not similarly attracted to employment with black firms.[17]

The National Insurance Association's 1963 convention addressed the issue of attracting white personnel. North Carolina Mutual's William A. Clement, the NIA's newly elected president, contended that unless black companies were successful in recruiting, selecting, training, and supervising other ethnic groups, ". . . we will be limited in penetrating the total market."[18] Despite Clement's exhortations, black companies were subsequently unable to attract significant numbers of prospective white employees and clients. Thus by 1967, Chicago Metropolitan, along with other NIA companies, had all but abandoned hopes of integrating its labor force.[19]

Chicago Metropolitan, despite disappointment over its inability to attract both white personnel and consumers, appeared to be an optimistic company during the 1960s. George S. Harris's (no relation to Thomas P. Harris) 1961 election as president contributed mightily to this hopefulness. His predecessor, Thomas P. Harris, had served as both chairman of the board and president since Robert A. Cole's death. The strain associated with the 1957 strike, along with increased competition from white firms, prompted Thomas P. Harris to share the responsibility of leading the company.

George S. Harris's ten-year presidency (1961–1971) corresponded with perhaps the most exciting years of recent African American history. The turbulent 1960s witnessed the evolution of both the Civil Rights and Black Power movements. George S. Harris, himself a long-time equal-rights advocate, made certain Chicago Metropolitan represented, to use the contemporary phrase, "part of the solution, rather than part of the problem." Despite the company's interest in gaining a share of the white consumer market, CMMAC remained committed to black community improvement during this period.

George S. Harris's first step toward better serving black Chicago was his enthusiastic support of CMMAC's Department of Research and Development, established in 1962. Headed by community activist and journalist Vernon Jarrett, this department's activities included: a widely circulated publication entitled *Urban Life,* which chronicled events of interest to both Chicago Metropolitan employees and the larger African American community; the establishment of an information bureau for residents of land clearance and urban renewal areas; and a concerted, yet ultimately unsuccessful drive to have March 5, the day of Crispus Attucks's 1770 death, designated as a national holiday.[20]

Besides attempting to solidify CMMAC's ties with the black community, George S. Harris sought to strengthen internal company pride and unity. Harris, during remarks directed to personnel at CMMAC's January 20, 1964, annual meeting, asserted:

> From this moment on, let no one among us look upon this company as some sort of stepping stone, a kind of training ground for some other job

somewhere else. I understand that this is the attitude of certain white companies, who are willing to let us go to the expense of training and preparing personnel, and then take them when we have completed this training. Look not at your company as a minor league outfit, where ambitious people prepare for the major leagues. Remember, we are Negroes and any insurance company that employs more than 500 people should not be considered minor league in our eyesight.[21]

Later in 1964, Harris established a Home Office Staff Committee which sought to duplicate the communications network employed during the company's early years.[22] This committee, which Harris later described as having ". . . solidified communications between upper and middle management, an aspect, that prior to the establishment of the Home Office Committee, was sorely lacking,"[23] further rejuvenated the company "family."

Despite the reinvigoration of company spirit under George S. Harris, the problem of increased white competition continued to plague Chicago Metropolitan. In late 1965, CMMAC, along with Supreme Life, attempted to address this problem in a definitive manner. In September officials from both black Chicago insurance companies formed an exploratory committee to examine the feasibility of a merger.[24] Previous discussions between CMMAC Chairman of the Board Thomas P. Harris and President Earl B. Dickerson of Supreme Life concluded that such a maneuver would result in ". . . a company of substance."[25] Despite initial enthusiasm concerning the proposed merger, by December 1965 all negotiations were terminated.[26] The major reason for the dissolution of merger negotiations between the two companies was an Illinois law that forbade the merger of a stock corporation (Supreme Life) and a mutual corporation (Chicago Metropolitan).[27] Moreover, some employees of both companies decried this proposal.[28]

The failure of these merger negotiations exacerbated the issue of white competition. Chicago Metropolitan personnel, like the vast majority of African Americans, applauded the dissolution of racial barriers. Still, it increasingly seemed that racial integration was a one-way street, consisting of black consumers and white-owned businesses getting together. It seemed ironic that white insurance companies, who for decades had discriminated against African Americans, were now profiting from increasing black socioeconomic mobility. From the standpoint of CMMAC, and black business in general, racial desegregation represented a bonanza for white entrepreneurs and a disaster for black ones.

Considering the apparent one-sided economic nature of 1960s racial desegregation, it is not surprising that Chicago Metropolitan and other black companies welcomed the development of "Black Power" sentiment during the mid-to-late 1960s. Although black businessmen represented "responsible" leadership, they, like the African American masses, did not benefit from racial desegregation. Consequently, while black businessmen abhorred the violence associated with Watts and other 1960s urban disorders, they nonetheless could identify with the frustration that led to these actions.

Chicago Metropolitan, led by President George S. Harris, stood at the forefront of black businesses' linkage with Black Power. Harris, elected NIA president in 1967,[29] became a noted national spokesman for African American economic self-determination. Harris's high visibility seemed especially significant, because he easily could have passed for white.

Speaking at CMMAC's January 16, 1967, annual meeting, Harris established the framework for the company's subsequent identification with the black pride and consciousness movements. Among his comments were:

> I speak of our company as a significant source of racial pride and hope in the context of our time. . . . We do not own steel mills; we do not own auto manufacturing plants; we do not own big clothing factories; we own no nationwide chains or dry goods or food stores; we own no cigarette or big beverage manufacturing companies; you can go down the line of strategic industries. While it can be explained easily as to why we are not elsewhere, it is a simple and obvious fact that the insurance business, our business, is the only sizable nationwide beachhead on the vast and rugged shores of big business. Chicago Metropolitan represents one of those beachheads . . . when this building was erected it was the pride of the Negro people of this city. . . . Racial pride was the prime ingredient that went into every inch of steel, bricks and mortar of this building. . . . Our job is to see to it that they [blacks] know about this company and what it means to them.[30]

Shortly thereafter, Vernon Jarrett, previously the head of CMMAC's Research and Development Department, became manager of a new Research and Publicity Department.[31] This new department, primarily concerned with public relations, sought to actively publicize the company's longtime community involvement. President George S. Harris, speaking at the January 15, 1968, annual meeting, offered the following justification for such a department:

> In Chicago alone there are a good million black people waiting to identify with *somebody*. They would prefer to identify with their own. . . . In a nutshell, we must re-educate, inform, and inspire the Negro community to the extent that when an agent rings a doorbell and says, "I'm from the Chicago Metropolitan Mutual Assurance Company," the potential policyholder answers, "Come on in. What took you so long?"[32] [Original emphasis]

Although CMMAC's Research and Publicity Department primarily sought to generate new business, the company's community outreach efforts were based upon more than financial considerations. The institution of a "Company Community Identification Program" in 1968 demonstrated this fact. This program, also coordinated by Vernon Jarrett, attempted to stimulate employee voluntary involvement in community organizations and activities.[33]

Chicago Metropolitan, besides its Research and Publicity Department and "Company Community Identification Program," also developed a widely distributed brochure entitled "Buy Black, Bank Black, Save Black, and Insure Black."[34] The company, moreover, was a prominent participant in Operation Breadbasket's* "Black Expo." This event featured the activities and accomplishments of African American business, political, and cultural organizations.[35]

Chicago Metropolitan's high profile during the late 1960s resulted in a steady increase of profitability (see table 6–2). The company, by actively promoting its longtime service to the black community, held its own against white competition. Still, while CMMAC took advantage of widespread black nationalist sentiment during this period, there existed a significant undercurrent of concern regarding the company's leadership.

An important characteristic of Chicago Metropolitan's early history was employees' long tenure of service. Since there was a dearth of white-collar positions available to African Americans during the first six decades of the twentieth century, many CMMAC employees spent considerable time with the company. Consequently, by the mid-1960s there was a preponderance of key personnel, many of them company pioneers, who had reached retirement age.

One definitive step taken to address this problem was Bowen M. Heffner's 1965 appointment to the post of vice-president / assistant to

---

*This 1960s Chicago-based organization, headed by the Rev. Jesse Jackson, served as a precursor to Operation PUSH.

TABLE 6–2
Selected Characteristics of Company Operations,
Chicago Metropolitan Mutual Assurance Company,
1964–1970

	Admitted *Assets*	Total Premium *Income*	Total Insurance *in Force*
1964	$18,240,000	$4,722,000	$138,442,000
1965	19,314,000	4,949,000	147,180,000
1966	20,609,000	5,123,000	155,403,000
1967	21,914,000	5,259,000	162,812,000
1968	23,124,000	5,713,000	172,855,000
1969	24,622,000	5,758,000	173,546,000
1970	25,921,000	5,910,000	179,169,000

Source: Best's Insurance Reports, 1969 *(Morristown, N.J.: A.M. Best Company, 1969) p. 272;* Best's 1974, *p. 309.*

the president.[36] Although Heffner himself was a longtime company employee (he joined the old MFSA in 1942), he was much younger than Thomas P. Harris, George S. Harris, Horace G. Hall, or James D. Grantham.

Besides Bowen Heffner's important promotion, Anderson M. Schweich's rise to prominence during the 1960s appeared especially significant. Schweich, who joined the company as the Accounting Department manager in 1951, possessed an extensive educational background in business administration, which included study at Loyola University of Chicago, Northwestern University, and Stanford University.[37] Schweich, who early on attracted Thomas P. Harris's favorable attention,[38] received a series of important promotions during the early 1960s.[39] By the mid-1960s, Schweich was vice-president/controller and a CMMAC board member.[40]

Chicago Metropolitan's Board of Directors, with Anderson Schweich, Bowen M. Heffner, and other younger personnel "waiting in the wings," established guidelines for mandatory retirement in December 1965. The board resolved that board members Thomas P. Harris, Horace G. Hall, James D. Grantham, Dr. Edward Beasley, and George S. Harris would be required to retire at age 70.[41] The board also agreed to make 65 the mandatory retirement age for future retirees ". . . regardless of rank, years of service, or other considerations."[42]

Despite these measures, the CMMAC board persuaded George S. Harris not to retire when he became eligible in 1968.[43] The board asked

Harris, whose personal style rejuvenated Chicago Metropolitan, to remain for the good of the company. While Harris agreed to continue, younger executives nonetheless assumed additional responsibilities. For instance, Anderson M. Schweich, George S. Harris's apparent successor, rose from vice-president/controller to executive vice-president in January 1969.[44]

In January 1970, Bowen M. Heffner and Warren H. Brothers were elected to the Board of Directors. (Brothers had served as CMMAC's actuary since 1958.) The administrative "youth movement" continued in February 1970 when Thomas P. Harris relinquished his position as general counsel to Hollis L. Green, Chicago Metropolitan's associate general counsel.[45]

By the end of 1970, Chicago Metropolitan's elderly leadership had identified and groomed several candidates for major roles in the company's future. Consequently, at a special February 11, 1971, Executive Committee meeting, the reins of authority were officially passed to a new generation. Among the major changes effected at this meeting were: Anderson M. Schweich would replace George S. Harris as president and James S. Isbell would become agency director, replacing Lorenzo D. Jones. Isbell, formerly with Chicago's Jackson Mutual, had been with CMMAC since 1955.[46] The Executive Committee also announced the official retirement of Thomas P. Harris, James D. Grantham, George S. Harris, Horace G. Hall, and Lorenzo D. Jones. These five individuals retained their board membership and each received a compensatory consulting position.[47]

Anderson M. Schweich's ascension to the CMMAC presidency marked a major milestone in the company's history. Schweich, unlike his predecessors, possessed an extensive academic and employment background in business administration. Consequently, Chicago Metropolitan, although unable to move fully into the mainstream of American business, began to more fully implement mainstream managerial and operational techniques.

Chairman of the Board Thomas P. Harris summarized Chicago Metropolitan's new direction during remarks at the January 17, 1972, annual meeting. Among other things, Harris asserted:

> We can no longer afford the luxury of pride in the number of black men and women who we have exposed to big business operations. . . . We can no longer glorify the millions of dollars we have contributed to the various community activities. . . . Established black business must lead the way by the test of profitability that is the yardstick by which all other

business is measured.... Undivided attention must be given to profitability with all other considerations being purely secondary.[48]

Anderson M. Schweich, like his immediate predecessors George S. Harris and Thomas P. Harris, faced the related problems of increased white competition and an inability to reach non-black consumers. Fortunately for Chicago Metropolitan, Schweich drew upon his considerable expertise and partially circumvented these obstacles. In December 1972, Schweich announced CMMAC would enter the group insurance field. Group insurance, which consists of a coverage agreement between an insurance company and a corporate employer, offered Chicago Metropolitan the prospect of additional business along with the opportunity to reach the elusive white consumer.[49] Among the first companies Chicago Metropolitan entered into group insurance agreements with were General Foods Corporation, Jewel Companies, Inc., and Commonwealth Edison.[50]

Besides CMMAC's entry into the group insurance market, the company's recruitment of Rumor L. Oden as agency training director represented another positive move. Oden, who joined Chicago Metropolitan in 1973, possessed considerable experience within the black insurance industry.[51] He, along with Agency Director James S. Isbell, subsequently molded the company's agency force into a unit that met President Schweich's expectations for personnel performance. During Isbell's tenure as agency director (1971–1980), the agency force reached the milestone of a $100,000 weekly premium income in both ordinary and industrial insurance.[52] Moreover, during Rumor Oden's ten years (1973–1983) as agency training director and director of manpower development, Chicago Metropolitan had the best ratio of persons passing the Illinois insurance license examination of any company in the state, black or white.[53]

Despite an upturn in profitability during Anderson M. Schweich's first years as president (see table 6–3), the mid-1970s were marked by stresses generated both inside and outside the company. Besides the recession of 1974–1975, which resulted in a noticeable drop in new policies issues (see table 6–4), 1975 witnessed the death of three long time CMMAC employees. In January, Melvin McNairy, former agency director and public relations director, passed away after a nearly 48-year association with the company.[54] Two months later, Rev. Dr. Richard C. Keller, CMMAC's chaplain for nearly thirty-eight years, died.[55] James Willard Tyler, Chicago Metropolitan's secretary and vice-chairman of the board,

TABLE 6–3
Selected Characteristics,
Chicago Metropolitan Mutual Assurance Company,
1971–1975

	Admitted Assets	Total Premium Income	Total Insurance in Force
1971	$26,985,000	$6,328,000	$190,551,000
1972	28,377,000	6,756,000	203,509,000
1973	29,762,000	7,398,000	394,566,000*
1974	31,237,000	7,995,000	426,850,000
1975	32,656,000	8,218,000	524,303,000

Source: Best's Insurance Reports, 1974 *(Morristown, N.J.: A.M. Best Company, 1974) p. 309;* Best's 1977, *p. 345.*

also expired in March 1975.[56] Chicago Metropolitan, as it had so often done in the past, rebounded from these difficulties and moved forward.

The company's mid-1970s healing process began with Hollis Green's selection as corporate secretary in March 1975.[57] It culminated in September 1976 with the selection of Weathers Y. Sykes as Chicago Metropolitan's senior vice-president/Administration.[58] "Sonny" Sykes, who had previously served in a variety of capacities at Supreme Life,[59] possessed considerable expertise in group life insurance.[60] The recession of 1974–1975, along with traditional African American underemployment, prompted CMMAC to place additional emphasis on group insurance, in lieu of concentrating solely on marketing individual and family policies.

The year 1977 marked the company's fiftieth anniversary as an incorporated entity. While CMMAC duly acknowledged the accomplishments of Robert A. Cole and other company pioneers,[61] 1977 also featured a recommendation to move Chicago Metropolitan's home office to another location. Alvin J. Boutte, newly elected board member and president of Chicago's black-owned Independence Bank, developed this proposal.

In March, Boutte, the first non-CMMAC employee elected to the company's Board of Directors,[62] approached President Schweich concerning a possible joint venture between Chicago Metropolitan and the

---

* The marked increase in CMMAC's total insurance in force beginning in 1973 reflected the company's growing involvement in the group insurance field.

TABLE 6–4
New Business Issued,
Chicago Metropolitan Mutual Assurance Company,
1974–1976

	Whole Life & *Endowment*	*Term*	*Industrial*
1974	$20,980,000	$9,324,000	$24,226,000
1975	19,374,000	5,904,000	21,832,000
1976	24,663,000	6,763,000	24,597,000

Source: Best's Insurance Reports: Life-Health, 1977 *(Oldwick, N.J.: A.M. Best Company, 1977) p. 345.*

Independence Bank. Specifically, Boutte proposed the construction of a combination black/insurance company office building in the 7900 block of South Cottage Grove Avenue.[63] Although CMMAC later financed a feasibility study for this project,[64] it never came to fruition.

Numerous company employees and community residents applauded Chicago Metropolitan's decision to remain at 4455 South King Drive. Many employees believed that leaving the northeast corner of 45th and King Drive would have been tantamount to dishonoring Robert A. Cole's legacy.[65] From the point of view of the company's immediate neighbors, CMMAC's decision to remain on King Drive represented a vote of confidence in Chicago's inner city. Since the early 1960s, with the advent of black residential mobility, many African American businessmen and professionals moved from central city locations to homes and offices further south. Consequently, 47th Street, once black Chicago's main commercial district, became a rundown shadow of its former self, catering to black Chicagoans financially unable to move. Chicago Metropolitan's decision to remain in the inner city offered encouragement and stability to a neighborhood badly in need of both.

While CMMAC's decision to remain at 4455 South King Drive reflected the company's continued commitment to working-class black Chicagoans, it did not preclude continued efforts to expand Chicago Met's consumer base. In 1977 Chicago Metropolitan began negotiations with members of Chicago's Hispanic community for the purpose of introducing the company to Spanish-speaking consumers.[66] These negotiations led to Chicago Metropolitan's training of several Hispanic agents.[67] Unfortunately for CMMAC these persons, once they received their licenses, abandoned Chicago Metropolitan. Apparently Hispanics, like whites, were reluctant to represent a black insurance company in their community.[68]

Although Chicago Metropolitan, during the 1960s and 1970s, experienced difficulty in attracting white and Hispanic personnel, the company compensated for this deficiency by fully utilizing the talents of African American females. During the early 1960s, the company removed its ban against female agents.[69] While this policy change generated early skepticism, CMMAC's new female agents rapidly won the respect of their male peers and supervisors.[70]

The 1968 selection of Irene Thompson as Chicago Metropolitan's top agent for the year marked an important milestone in company history. Thompson's efforts, which also earned her special recognition from the National Insurance Association,[71] proved beyond a doubt that women could be effective insurance agents. In recent years, it appears the question is not whether women can be agents, but whether they are better agents than men. For instance, in 1983 Herbert W. Cooley, then Chicago Met's assistant vice-president / field service officer, made the following observation, after announcing that Lillie Garrett would represent CMMAC as its top agent at the 1983 NIA convention:

> What has happened *fellows* to our competitive spirit and desire to be big earners? It seems that most of our *salesmen* have taken up with the drift of the times and will not extend themselves to be achievers. We do have a *new breed* at Chicago Met and they seem to be taking over the leadership role; they are the *ladies* of our agency force.[72] (Emphasis his)

Besides significant gains made by women in CMMAC's Agency Department, Josephine King's rise to prominence also reflected women's changing status within the company. King, who joined CMMAC in 1959 as a file clerk in the Data Processing Department, by the late 1980s stood as vice-president/Administration and a board member.[73] Her success appears to have been based upon hark work coupled with encouragement from President Anderson M. Schweich, her longtime mentor.[74] Schweich early on advised King to undertake training with the Life Office Management Association (LOMA). This organization offers courses relating to insurance company management and administers a series of examinations to determine trainees' proficiency. Once a candidate passes all exams, he or she becomes a Fellow of the Life Management Institute and receives the prestigious FLMI designation.[75]

In 1976, Josephine King became the first CMMAC female to earn FLMI designation.[76] Consequently her status within the company, as well as within the insurance industry, rose accordingly. In 1980, King became senior vice-president/Administration.[77] That same year, the Chicago chapter of the National Association of Insurance Women International (NAIW) elected King president. She was the first black president in the chapter's then 41-year history.[78]

Despite Josephine King's impressive achievements, she does not hold the distinction of being Chicago Metropolitan's first female board member. Dorothy McConner, vice-president/Administration and corporate secretary of the Johnson Products Company, became a board member in January 1980, preceding Josephine King by two years.[79] McConner, chosen to replace the retiring Warren H. Brothers,[80] had an impressive career at Johnson Products, a Chicago-based black hair care firm. Her status, as both an "outsider" and a woman, added a fresh perspective to Chicago Metropolitan's administrative deliberations.[81]

While the company made progress in such areas as female workers' status and group insurance, an undercurrent of employee discontent existed during Anderson M. Schweich's first years as president. Schweich, similar to Thomas P. Harris, suffered the misfortune of succeeding an extremely popular president. Although George S. Harris appeared not as beloved as Robert A. Cole, he was nonetheless a dynamic individual who enjoyed contact with company personnel. Schweich, while equally dynamic, adopted a more detached administrative style. Schweich's apparent aloofness, coupled with CMMAC's growing emphasis on corporate efficiency, caused several longtime employees to fear that Chicago Metropolitan's traditional family atmosphere seemed in danger of extinction.[82]

At CMMAC's January 19, 1981, annual meeting, Schweich squarely addressed the issue of company morale. He noted an apparent loss of some of the "close-knit family relationship" that characterized Chicago Metropolitan over the years. He further lamented that this loss of morale appeared to have a negative impact on company operations.[83]

It appears that Schweich's concern over employee morale partially influenced Chicago Metropolitan's mid-1981 decision to renovate its 4455 South King Drive home office.[84] The multimillion-dollar renovation, completed in 1985, rejuvenated company spirit and reaffirmed Robert A. Cole's legacy. Still Chicago Metropolitan, despite excitement concerning its renovated headquarters, remained in the midst of a serious economic challenge.

Although Chicago Metropolitan entered the lucrative group insurance market during the 1970s, it, along with other black insurance companies, continued to compete unsuccessfully with white insurance companies. During the 1960s, gaining access to the mainstream consumer market was Chicago Metropolitan's chief concern. During the 1970s and 1980s, the issue of product variety joined limited access to consumers as a major marketing problem.

Chicago Metropolitan and other black companies, because they are restricted to a single market (and a relatively impoverished one at that), historically have been small operations with limited capital for corporate research. On the other hand, Prudential, Metropolitan Life, and other industry giants have considerably more resources to develop new products and marketing strategies. Consequently, during the mid-1970s, mainstream companies, sensing the market was right, began to offer consumers both qualified advice on retirement strategies and other investments.[85]

Data from the authoritative *Best's Reports* for the years 1978–1985 illustrates both the success of the mainstream insurance industry's "new direction" and the simultaneous decline of black insurance companies. As tables 6–5 and 6–6 indicate, between 1978 and 1985 the number of black firms listed in *Best's* compilation of the 500 leading life insurance companies dropped from six to two. Moreover, the average premium income growth of the two remaining African American companies compared unfavorably to the industry average. Between 1978 and 1985, all U.S. and Canadian life insurance companies experienced a 10.5 percent increase in premium income.[86] During the same period, North Carolina Mutual and Golden State Mutual, the top black companies, had premium income growth of only 4.2 percent and 3.6 percent, respectively.[87] When the years 1984–1985 are examined, the discrepancy appeared even greater. While all U.S. and Canadian companies had a 15.1 percent increase of premium income during this two-year period, North Carolina Mutual had a 0.9 percent *decrease* in premium income and Golden State registered a small 1.2 percent gain.[88]

Besides competition from diversified mainstream companies, black companies in the 1970s and 1980s were threatened by attempts to outlaw industrial insurance. The campaign to eliminate industrial insurance, the bedrock of the African American insurance industry, began with a mid-1978 Federal Trade Commission investigation.[89] This probe led to a widely read November 1978 *Consumer Reports* article entitled "Insurance That Preys on the Poor."[90] *Consumer Reports,* after comparing industrial

TABLE 6–5
Ranking of the Top Six African American Insurance Companies*
within *Best's* Listing of the 500 Leading Life Insurance
Companies in Total Premium Income, 1978–1981

	1978	*1979*	*1980*	*1981*
North Carolina Mutual	195	204	211	240
Golden State Mutual	306	324	336	357
Atlanta Life	362	369	387	415
Universal Life	389	398	424	440
Supreme Life	421	406	454	473
Chicago Metropolitan	492	494	—	—

Source: Best's Review: Life/Health Insurance Edition, *80 (August 1979), pp. 35–38; 81 (August 1980), pp. 39–42; 82 (September 1981), pp. 71–74; 83 (September 1982), pp. 44–47.*

insurance to whole life and term coverage, concluded: "In our judgement, state legislatures should enact a ban on any further sales of industrial (weekly premium) insurance. Anyone so poor as to need the weekly collection system would almost certainly be better off without the product."[91]

Shortly after *Consumer Reports'* damning appraisal of industrial insurance, the National Association of Insurance Commissioners established a task force on home service (industrial) insurance. This group's findings were published in a December 1982 report entitled *Home Service Life Insurance: A Commentary.* The task force, despite growing criticism of industrial insurance, concluded that it ". . . served a useful social function."[92]

Chicago Metropolitan and other black insurance companies were encouraged by the Home Service Insurance Task Force's findings. Still, they realized that critics of industrial insurance raised several valid points. For instance, *Consumer Reports* demonstrated that term and monthly debit ordinary (MDO) policies were much more economical than weekly industrial policies.[93] Another acknowledged deficiency of industrial insurance policies was their relatively low face value. Numerous elderly industrial insurance policyholders have paid more in premiums over the years than the policy's cash value.[94]

---

*North Carolina Mutual is based in Durham, North Carolina; Golden State Mutual is based in Los Angeles, California; Atlanta Life is based in Atlanta, Georgia; Universal Life is based in Memphis, Tennessee; and Supreme Life is based in Chicago, Illinois.

TABLE 6–6

**Ranking of the Top Six African American Insurance Companies
within *Best's* Listing of the 500 Leading Life Insurance
Companies in Total Premium Income,* 1982–1985**

	1982	*1983*	*1984*	*1985*
North Carolina Mutual	262	271	289	307
Golden State Mutual	388	406	433	448
Atlanta Life	451	479	—	—
Universal Life	495	—	—	—
Supreme Life	—	—	—	—
Chicago Metropolitan	—	—	—	—

Source: Best's Review: Life/Health Insurance Edition, *84 (August 1983), pp. 46–49; 85
(July 1984), pp. 76–79; 86 (August 1985), pp. 66–69; 87 (July 1986), pp. 25–28.*

Widespread discussion concerning the shortcomings of industrial
insurance, along with increasing competition from white companies
(who generally had long abandoned industrial insurance), forced Chicago Metropolitan and other black companies to consider phasing out
industrial insurance altogether. Consequently, in July 1985 when *Black
Enterprise* magazine saluted Chicago Metropolitan's home office renovation, it also commended the company's plans for expanding its insurance
portfolio. Among the new policies CMMAC intended to market were
single-premium term insurance and joint whole life / whole mortgage
coverage, which catered to married couples who wanted to pay a single
premium for a joint whole life or mortgage package.[95]

Although the July 1985 *Black Enterprise* article seemed confident in
tone, conditions within CMMAC's Agency Department were less than
ideal. Chicago Metropolitan, besides problems related to stiff white
competition, also suffered from Agency Department instability. After
Jack Isbell's 1980 promotion from vice-president / agency director to
senior vice-president / Corporate Development,[96] it took more than two
years to appoint another agency director. While President Schweich
praised Edward J. Halfacre's December 1982 appointment as vice-president / director of marketing,[97] his subsequent term as agency director
proved less than illustrious. Halfacre, previously with the North Carolina
Mutual Life Insurance Company, almost immediately aroused the ani-

---

**Best's Review* lists only U.S. and Canadian companies.

mus of agents.[98] In addition to his abrasive personality, which alienated many agents, Halfacre was a sickly man whose chronic illness forced him to resign in 1985.[99]

John E. Fitzpatrick's November 1985 appointment as agency director appeared to restore stability to CMMAC's Agency Department. Fitzpatrick, who joined Chicago Metropolitan as an agent in 1955, seemed fully aware of the unique characteristics of company agency operations.[100] Moreover, because Fitzpatrick represented "home grown" talent, he did not attract the agent mistrust directed at such "outsiders" as Lorenzo D. Jones and Edward J. Halfacre. Considering that CMMAC's future rested squarely on the Agency Department's performance, Fitzpatrick's well-received promotion enhanced company morale at a crucial juncture in Chicago Metropolitan's history.

Still, despite this resurgence of company esprit de corps, by the mid-1980s Chicago Metropolitan remained at a competitive disadvantage to powerful mainstream companies. Consequently, despite the home office renovation and John Fitzpatrick's popular elevation, there were some CMMAC personnel who viewed the company's future as extremely tenuous. Unfortunately, from the perspective of the Chicago Metropolitan Mutual Assurance Company, subsequent events verified this sense of foreboding.

VII

EPILOGUE

It appears that the completed 1985 renovation of Chicago Metropolitan's home office complex represented the last high point of the company's history. Continuing pressure from white-owned companies, along with the growing unemployment of working-class blacks (the company's chief constituency), had a devastating effect on company operations. By 1990 Chicago Metropolitan, faced with possible dissolution by the Illinois Department of Insurance, agreed to a friendly acquisition by the black-owned Atlanta Life Insurance Company. Moreover, Chicago Metropolitan's fate represented a microcosm of the increasingly uncertain world of black insurance companies.

On November 9, 1990, the policyholders of the Chicago Metropolitan Mutual Assurance Company held, perhaps, the most important meeting in company history. The purpose of this gathering was to approve the company's reorganization from a mutual insurance company (owned by policyholders) to a stock insurance company. In addition, CMMAC policyholders were asked to approve the purchase of all subsequent stock by the Atlanta Life Insurance Company, thus making Chicago Metropolitan a wholly-owned subsidiary of Atlanta Life. Chicago Metropolitan's Board of Directors, which approved the proposed reorganization at its August 15, 1990, meeting, unanimously urged CMMAC policyholders to do likewise.[1]

Mounting problems associated with Chicago Metropolitan's mortgage loans and real estate holdings led to this disturbing scenario. During most of the 1980s, Chicago Metropolitan received a rating of "C+" (which denoted a "fairly good" insurance company) from the authoritative *Best's Insurance Reports*.[2] Yet, in its examination of Chicago Metropolitan's operations during 1989, the 1990 edition of *Best's* gave the company a rating of "NA-7," or "below minimum standards." *Best's* apparently based its judgment on the fact that Chicago Met experienced a 61% decline in capital and surplus funds "due mainly to substantial unrealized capital losses reported from the mortgage and real estate portfolios."[3]

Chicago Metropolitan, like most of the other six top black companies, listed mortgages as a significant proportion of its admitted assets (see table 7–1). This reflected black insurance companies' historic role of providing mortgage loans to working-class African Americans. Yet, because mortgage loans are profitable only when employed home buyers consistently pay their house notes, accelerated African American unemployment during the 1980s posed still another threat to Chicago Metropolitan and other black insurance companies. As Andrew Hacker noted in *Two Nations: Black and White, Separate, Hostile, Unequal:*

> Since 1974, unemployment rates for blacks have remained at double-digit levels, and they have not fallen below twice the white rate since 1976. Even more depressing, the gap between the black and white figures grew during the 1980s, suggesting that the economy has little interest in enlisting black contributions.[4]

In Chicago, late 1980s census data verified the presence of two separate and unequal racial enclaves within the city limits. For example, by 1989, twenty-five years after the passage of the Civil Rights Act of 1964, the African American per capita income of $8,569 represented a mere 47% of European Americans' per capita income of $18,258.[5] At the same time, 33.2 percent of black Chicagoans, as compared to 11.0 percent of white Chicagoans, had incomes below the poverty level.[6]

TABLE 7–1

Percentage of Admitted Assets in Mortgage Loans,
the Six Leading Black Insurance Companies, 1989

North Carolina Mutual (Durham, N.C.)	21
Atlanta Life (Atlanta, Ga.)	2
Golden State Mutual (Los Angeles, Calif.)	41
Universal Life Insurance Co. (Memphis, Tenn.)	24
Supreme Life (Chicago, Ill.)	4
Chicago Metropolitan (Chicago, Ill.)	26

Source: Black Enterprise *20 (June 1990), pp. 210–11;* Best's Insurance Reports: Life/ Health Edition *85 (1990), pp. 304, 496, 980, 1674, 2136, 2325.*

Besides its negative impact on Chicago Metropolitan's mortgage loan program, black Chicago's economic decline during the 1980s adversely affected the company's premium income. Between 1984 and 1989, annual new insurance issued dropped from $30,536,000 to $24,395,000.[7]

By contrast, Atlanta Life managed to reasonably withstand the pressures put upon black America by the Reagan administration. Atlanta Life's success appeared linked to its historical tradition of prudent conservatism. Unlike the free-wheeling Robert A. Cole, Alonzo F. Herndon, Atlanta Life's founder, personified caution and stability.[8] Herndon's influence, as evidenced by tables 7–1 and 7–2, continues to this day. While Atlanta Life, among black insurance companies, has the smallest percentage of admitted assets in mortgage loans, its percentage of admitted assets in stocks and bonds exceeds that of the other top black firms.

Another Atlanta Life tradition, taking over the operations of distressed black firms,[9] also continued to manifest itself during the 1980s. In 1985, Atlanta Life merged with the Mammoth Life and Accident Company of Louisville, Kentucky. Two years later, Atlanta Life purchased the Southern Aid Life Insurance Company of Richmond, Virginia.[10] Still, Atlanta Life's 1990 acquisition of Chicago Metropolitan represented a truly monumental event in both companies' recent histories.

On January 1, 1991, the Chicago Metropolitan Mutual Assurance Company ceased to exist. In its place, in accordance with the demutualization and sale of the company, stood the Chicago Metropolitan Assurance Company.[11] Besides the name change, the reorganized company's Board of Directors assumed a new look. Out of twelve board members, only three

TABLE 7–2
**Percentage of Admitted Assets in Stocks and Bonds,
the Six Leading Black Insurance Companies, 1989**

	Stocks	*Bonds*	*Total*
North Carolina Mutual	1	48	49
Atlanta Life	11	65	76
Golden State Mutual	2	35	37
Universal Life	12	53	65
Supreme Life	0.2	66	66.2
Chicago Metropolitan	10	44	54

Source: Black Enterprise *20 (June 1990), pp. 210–11;* Best's Insurance Reports: Life/ Health Edition *85 (1990), pp. 304, 496, 980, 1674, 2136, 2325.*

former Chicago Met board members (Anderson Schweich, Josephine King, and Alvin Boutte) were retained.[12]

At the same time Chicago Metropolitan experienced this dramatic restructuring, its South Side rival, the Supreme Life Insurance Company, also found itself in severe financial difficulty. However, unlike Chicago Metropolitan, Supreme Life ultimately ceded its insurance operations to a white-owned firm.

As early as 1981 Supreme Life began receiving a rating of "NA-7" by *Best's Insurance Reports*.[13] Chief among Supreme's problems were above-average lapse rates (no doubt caused by worsening economic conditions among African Americans) and significant real estate losses.[14] In fact, between 1985 and 1990 Supreme Life wrote off nearly $4 million in bad real estate loans.[15]

By 1991 Supreme Life, facing mounting lapse rates, growing real estate losses, and declining new business (see table 7–3), had to seriously reevaluate its operations. Seeing no other viable alternative, the company sold the vast majority of its admitted assets to the white-owned United Insurance Company of America.[16] Supreme Life's chairman of the board, John H. Johnson, had wanted to sell his company's assets to black-owned insurance companies. Yet because Supreme Life's loan portfolios were problematic, other African American insurance companies were justifiably unwilling to assume additional undue risk and backed away.[17]

Chicago Metropolitan's loss of autonomy and Supreme Life's sale to a white-owned company vividly illustrate the tenuous position of African American insurance companies in contemporary America. In fact, this

TABLE 7–3
New Business Generated,
Supreme Life Insurance Company,
1984–1989

1984	$34,060,000
1985	39,990,000
1986	38,834,000
1987	40,124,000
1988	27,305,000
1989	17,520,000

Source: Best's Insurance Reports: Life/Health Edition *85 (1990), p. 2137.*

historic cornerstone of black economic development appears to be crumbling before our very eyes.

Black Enterprise's June 1989 annual overview of the black insurance industry graphically set the tone for this new reality. In large, bold letters, *Black Enterprise* informed its readers that black insurers had two options: **FORTIFY OR DIE.**[18] Within three years of this ominous forecast, four large black-owned companies (including Chicago Metropolitan and Supreme Life) had been sold to larger black or white firms. In 1989, Atlanta Life purchased the Pilgrim Health and Life Insurance Company of Augusta, Georgia. Pilgrim, before its sale, had been the ninth largest black insurance company in the United States.[19] In 1992, the Harlem-based United Life Insurance Company, because of increased business pressure, agreed to be absorbed by the giant Metropolitan Life Insurance Company.[20]

Despite the troubles of some black insurance companies, others (most notably the top three companies) have sought to fortify their operations. North Carolina Mutual, the largest black insurer, has diversified its operations to include pension fund advisory services and real estate management.[21] Atlanta Life, as demonstrated through its acquisition of Chicago Metropolitan and other firms, has fortified itself through mergers.[22] Finally, the Golden State Mutual Life Insurance Company of Los Angeles has enhanced its image by creating new products aimed at

TABLE 7–4

Ranking of the Top Three African American Insurance Companies within Best's Listing of the 500 Leading Life Insurance Companies in Total Premium Income, 1986–1992

	1986	1987	1988	1989	1990	1991	1992
North Carolina Mutual	310	328	345	387	383	404	416
Atlanta Life	491	—	—	—	—	—	—
Golden State Mutual	442	454	481	—	497	—	—

Source: Best's Review: Life/Health Insurance Edition, *88 (August 1987), pp. 99–103; 89 (August 1988), pp. 105–10; 90 (July 1989), pp. 78–84; 91 (July 1990), pp. 14–20; 92 (July 1991), pp. 19–24; 94 (July 1993), pp. 25–32.*

African American professionals. Moreover, in 1988 Golden State signed then–Dallas Cowboy running back Herschel Walker as a celebrity spokesman. In the short term, Walker's fame gave Golden State Mutual additional visibility.[23]

Despite the recent efforts of America's three largest African American insurance companies to remain competitive, current trends suggest a rough road ahead for them and their smaller counterparts. Table 7–4 clearly suggests the steady decline of North Carolina Mutual, Atlanta Life, and Golden State Mutual relative to the entire insurance industry. For example, by 1992 only North Carolina Mutual remained in the *Best's* listing of the top 500 insurance companies in premium income. Moreover, considering NCM's steady drop in rank, it seems very plausible that by the year 2000 (if not before) there will not be an African American firm listed among the industry leaders.

As Chicago Metropolitan (now a division of Atlanta Life) and other African American insurance companies move toward the twenty-first century, their collective future appears uncertain. Still, regardless of what happens, one thing remains clear and undisputable. The history of Chicago Metropolitan, and other black insurance companies, deserves respect and recognition.

NOTES

Introduction

1. During the 1950s, this Illinois-domiciled company expanded into Indiana and Missouri. See chapter 3 for details.

2. Horace R. Cayton and St. Clair Drake, *Black Metropolis: A Study of Negro Life in a Northern City* (New York: Harcourt, Brace, & World, 1970; originally published in 1945). This magisterial work remains, fifty years after its initial publication, perhaps the most in-depth study of an African American enclave.

3. Arnold R. Hirsch, *Making the Second Ghetto: Race and Housing in Chicago, 1940–1960* (New York: Cambridge University Press, 1983), p. 17.

4. Carter G. Woodson, "Insurance Business among Negroes," *Journal of Negro History,* 14 (1929), pp. 202–12; Merah S. Stuart, *An Economic Detour: A History of Insurance in the Lives of American Negroes* (College Park, MD: McGrath, 1969; originally published in 1940), pp. 11–34; John Sibley Butler, *Entrepreneurship and Self-Help among Black Americans* (Albany: State University of New York Press, 1991), p. 109.

5. There have been four book-length studies of individual African American insurance companies: Jesse L. Gloster, *North Carolina Mutual Life Insurance Company: Its Historical Development and Current Operations* (New York: Arno, 1976; reprint of Ph.D. dissertation, University of Pittsburgh, 1955); Robert C. Puth, *Supreme Life: The History of a Negro Life Insurance Company* (New York: Arno, 1976; reprint of Ph.D. dissertation, Northwestern University, 1968); Walter B. Weare, *Black Business in the New South: A Social History of the North Carolina Mutual Life Insurance Company* (Urbana: University of Illinois Press, 1973); and Alexa Benson Henderson, *Atlanta Life Insurance Company: Guardian of Black Economic Dignity* (Tuscaloosa: University of Alabama Press, 1990).

6. Stuart, *An Economic Detour,* pp. 72–89, 117–29, 196–213.

7. See chapter 1 for a discussion of Daniel Jackson's and Robert A. Cole's gambling activities.

8. There have been several studies which have discussed the mainstream insurance industry's changing attitudes toward African Americans during the late nineteenth century. They include: Harry H. Pace, "The Attitude of Life Insurance Companies toward Negroes," *Southern Workman,* 57 (January 1928), pp. 3–7; Carter G. Woodson, "Insurance Business among Negroes," *Journal of Negro History,* 14 (1929), pp. 202–26; William J. Trent, "Development of Negro Life Insurance Companies," M.A. thesis, University of Pennsylvania, 1932, pp. 24–28; George M. Fredrickson, *The Black Image in the White Mind: The Debate on African American Character and Destiny, 1817–1914* (Middletown, CT: Wesleyan University Press, 1971), pp. 246–55.

9. Butler, *Entrepreneurship and Self-Help among Black Americans,* p. 122.

10. Stuart, *An Economic Detour,* pp. xxii–xxiv.

11. Ibid., p. 37.

12. Ibid.

13. Ibid., pp. 37–38.

14. Between 1939 and 1941, the life expectancy of black males was 52.3 years and 62.8 years for white males. Between 1949 and 1951, the figures were 58.9 and 66.3, respectively. The comparative figures for females equally demonstrated life expectancy gains for African Americans. Between 1939 and 1941, the life expectancy for black females was 55.5 years and 67.3 for white females. Between 1949 and 1951, the figures were 62.7 and 72.0. Moreover, between 1959 and 1961, the life expectancy of black males was 61.5 years and 67.6 for white males. Among females, the figures stood at 66.5 for blacks and 74.2 for whites. See *The Social and Economic Status of the Black Population in the United States: A Historical View, 1790–1978* (Washington, DC: Bureau of the Census, 1979), p. 120.

15. Robert H. Kinzer and Edward Sagarin, *The Negro in American Business: The Conflict between Separatism and Integration* (New York: Greenberg, 1950), pp. 100–101.

16. Ibid.

17. Puth, *Supreme Life,* p. 50.

18. Ibid., pp. 276–77.

19. Linda P. Fletcher, *The Negro in the Insurance Industry* (Philadelphia: University of Pennsylvania Press, 1970), p. 129.

20. *Best's Review,* the authoritative insurance industry publication which ranks insurance companies according to their premium income, reveals a dramatic recent erosion in the status of African American insurance companies. (See tables 6–5, 6–6, and 7–5.)

21. Weare, *Black Business in the New South,* p. 280.

22. Ibid., pp. 280–81.

23. Henderson, *Atlanta Life,* pp. 204, 206.

24. See chapter 6 for a discussion of the problems black insurance companies have had since the 1960s trying to reach non-black consumers.

25. Interview, Weathers Y. Sykes, April 15, 1986. Mr. Sykes, now deceased, joined Chicago Metropolitan in 1976 in the capacity of senior vice-president/Administration. Also, see Roger Barnes, "Shotgun Mergers (Insurance Overview)," *Black Enterprise,* 20 (June 1990), pp. 205–206.

1. The Metropolitan Funeral System Association, 1925–1946

1. Unidentified manuscript and author, Illinois Writers Project, The Negro in Illinois Series, Folder MSS IWP 20, Vivian Harsh Collection, Carter G. Woodson Regional Library, Chicago, Illinois.

2. Chicago Commission on Race Relations, *The Negro in Chicago: A Study of Race Relations and a Race Riot* (Chicago: University of Chicago Press, 1922), p. 3. Some migrants, because of the sheer size of the "Great Migration" to Chicago, did settle (with hardship) in previously all-white areas.

3. Harrison L. Harris, Jr., "Negro Mortality in Chicago," *Social Service Review,* 1 (1927), pp. 58–60.

4. Robert C. Puth, *Supreme Life: The History of a Negro Life Insurance Company* (New York: Arno, 1976; reprint of Ph.D. dissertation, Northwestern University, 1968), p. 26.

5. Interview, Lee L. Bailey, May 16, 1986. Mr. Bailey began working with Chicago Metropolitan in 1928. He is considered the company "griot."

6. Harold F. Gosnell, *Negro Politicians: The Rise of Negro Politics in Chicago* (Chicago: University of Chicago Press, 1935), pp. 130–33; Chicago *Defender,* May 18, 1929, p. 1.

7. John Sibley Butler, *Entrepreneurship and Self-Help among Black Americans* (Albany: SUNY Press, 1991), pp. 109–10.

8. Gosnell, *Negro Politicians,* p. 132.

9. Ibid., p. 131.

10. Lee L. Bailey, May 16, 1986.

11. Ibid.

12. Ibid.

13. Gosnell, *Negro Politicians,* p. 132.

14. Lee L. Bailey, May 16, 1986.

15. Chicago *Tribune,* July 9, 1955, p. 8; Chicago *Defender,* December 12, 1942, p. 15.

16. Ibid.

17. Lee L. Bailey, May 16, 1986.

18. Chicago *Defender,* May 26, 1945, p. 3; interview, Ann Childs, August 4, 1986. Mrs. Childs is Ahmad A. Rayner's daughter.

19. Minutes, Organizational Meeting, Metropolitan Funeral System Association, December 19, 1927.

20. Ibid.

21. Horace R. Cayton and St. Clair Drake, *Black Metropolis: A Study of Negro Life in a Northern City* (New York: Harcourt, Brace, 1945), p. 223.

22. *A Place in the Sun: A Pictorial and Graphic Review of the Rise of the Metropolitan Funeral System Association* (Chicago: Metropolitan Funeral System Association, 1930), no pagination; obituary, Rev. Mansfield Edward Bryant Peck, May 20, 1946. Rev. Peck, whose church affiliation was the Greater Bethel A.M.E. Church, also advised church members to join MFSA.

23. Illinois Department of Insurance Examination of the MFSA, November 24, 1931, pp. 6–7. According to this survey of company operations, MFSA had attracted 70,000 policyholders by 1929.

24. Burial Records, Metropolitan Funeral System Association, August 29, 1926, to December 11, 1928. The occupations of deceased MFSA males that could be considered professional, skilled, or proprietary were: mechanic (4); tailor (3); farmer/retired (1); decorator (1); minister (1); stationary fireman (1); grocer (1); plumber (1); police officer (1); and newsdealer (1). The occupations of deceased females that could be considered professional, skilled, or proprietary were: seamstress (1); hair dresser (1); and insurance agent (1).

25. Illinois Department of Insurance Examination of the MFSA, November 24, 1931, p. 4.

26. Ibid.

27. Ibid., p. 15.

28. Lee L. Bailey, May 16, 1986.

29. Minutes, Executive Committee Meeting, MFSA, September 9, 1929.

30. Minutes, General Membership (Policyholders) Meeting, MFSA, June 24, 1929.

31. Minutes, General Meeting, MFSA, December 23, 1929.

32. MFSA, *A Place in the Sun,* no pagination.

33. "Black Metropolis Historic District," Proposal Submitted to the Commission on Chicago Historical and Architectural Landmarks, March 7, 1984, p. 5.

34. Chicago *Defender,* March 1, 1930, p. 3.

35. Ibid.

36. Lee L. Bailey, May 16, 1986.

37. Chicago *Defender,* July 23, 1932, p. 2.

38. Ernest W. Burgess Papers, Box 133, Folder 1, Department of Special Collections, Joseph Regenstein Library, University of Chicago.

39. Ibid.

40. Associated Negro Press, news release, December 19, 1932, Claude A. Barnett Papers, Chicago Historical Society.

41. Lee L. Bailey, May 16, 1986.

42. MFSA, *A Place in the Sun,* no pagination.

43. Minutes, MFSA General Meeting, December 23, 1929.

44. Associated Negro Press, news release, December 19, 1932, Claude A. Barnett Papers.

45. Cayton and Drake, *Black Metropolis,* pp. 526–63.

46. Interview, Earl B. Dickerson, November 26, 1986. Dickerson, besides serving on the legal team that defended MFSA against Charles Jackson's charges, later served as a city alderman and president of the Supreme Life Company.

47. Minutes, MFSA General Meeting, December 23, 1929.

48. Illinois Department of Insurance Examination of the MFSA, November 24, 1931, pp. 10, 14.

49. Minutes, General Meeting, MFSA, December 23, 1929.

50. Interview, Jesse L. Moman, March 6, 1986. Mr. Moman, among other things, coordinated the writing of a brief company history in 1977.

51. Illinois Department of Insurance Examination of the MFSA, June 10, 1932, p. 6.

52. State Charter of the System Burial Company, June 6, 1932.

53. Minutes, General Meeting, MFSA, January 15, 1934.

54. Lee L. Bailey, May 16, 1986; Ford S. Black, *Black's Blue Book, 1921* (Chicago: self-published, 1921), p. 65.

55. Lee L. Bailey, May 16, 1986. Mr. Bailey was one of the agents approached by Nelson.

56. Minutes, General Meeting, MFSA, January 16, 1939.

57. Ibid.

58. "Black Metropolis Historic District," p. 5.

59. Cayton and Drake, *Black Metropolis,* pp. 88, 214–18.

60. Marquis James, *The Metropolitan Life: A Study in Business Growth* (New York: Viking, 1947), pp. 279–80; Walter B. Weare, *Black Business in the New South: A Social History of the North Carolina Mutual Life Insurance Company* (Urbana: University of Illinois Press, 1973), pp. 159–60.

61. Interview, Dorothy Harper, December 4, 1985 (Mrs. Harper is Fred W. Lewing's daughter). Lee L. Bailey, May 16, 1986.

62. Lee L. Bailey, May 16, 1986.

63. Ibid.

64. Dorothy Harper, December 4, 1985; interview, Robert F. Jones, June 27, 1986. Mr. Jones joined the company as an agent in 1933 and worked for Chicago Metropolitan until 1967.

65. Lee L. Bailey, May 16, 1986.

66. Illinois Department of Insurance Examination of the MFSA, November 24, 1931, p. 4.

67. Ibid., pp. 6–7; Illinois Department of Insurance Examination of the MFSA, December 7, 1933, p. 13.

68. James, *Metropolitan Life,* p. 325; Winfred O. Bryson, Jr. "Negro Life Insurance Companies: A Comparative Analysis of the Operating and Financial Experience of Negro Legal Reserve Life Insurance Companies," Ph.D. dissertation, University of Pennsylvania, 1948, p. 75.

69. Minutes, MFSA General Meeting, January 15, 1934.
70. Chicago Metropolitan Mutual Assurance Company Executive Roster, 1960.
71. Ibid.
72. Minutes, Board of Directors Meeting, MFSA, January 15, 1934.
73. Cayton and Drake, *Black Metropolis,* pp. 258–59.
74. MFSA, *A Place in the Sun,* no pagination; Jesse L. Moman, September 24, 1985; interview, Leon Sanders, May 27, 1986. Mr. Sanders joined the company in 1942 and worked until 1975.
75. MFSA, *A Place in the Sun,* no pagination.
76. Ibid.
77. Minutes, General Meeting, MFSA, January 18, 1937. Lautier lost by a vote of 90–56 (39 of her votes were by proxy). A woman would not sit on the company's Board of Directors until 1980.
78. Robert A. Cole to Ernest Palmer, director of the Illinois Department of Insurance, October 22, 1937.
79. Illinois Department of Insurance Examination of the MFSA, November 24, 1931, pp. 5–6.
80. Minutes, Board Meeting, MFSA, December 13, 1931.
81. Minutes, Board Meeting, MFSA, July 1, 1935.
82. Ibid.
83. Robert A. Cole to Ernest Palmer, October 22, 1937.
84. Ernest Palmer to MFSA, December 22, 1937.
85. Robert A. Cole to Ernest Palmer, April 7, 1938.
86. Ernest Palmer to Robert A. Cole, April 8, 1938.
87. Cayton and Drake, *Black Metropolis,* pp. 450–51.
88. Dorothy Harper, December 4, 1985. Mrs. Malone's "PORO System" and "PORO Colleges" in St. Louis and Chicago, represented significant competition to Madame C. J. Walker, the leading figure in the early twentieth century black (women's) beauty culture. Walker, whose real name was Sarah Breedlove, was an African American entrepreneur who perfected the "hot comb," a device used to straighten black women's hair. She also invented various complexion creams and hair pomades. The legacy of Madame C. J. Walker and Annie Malone remains strong. Today, the African American personal care industry is a multi-billion-dollar enterprise. See Darlene Clark Hine, et al., eds., *Black Women in America: An Historical Encyclopedia,* volume II, pp. 1209–13.
89. MFSA to Ernest Palmer, August 16, 1939.
90. Ibid.
91. Minutes, Board Meeting, MFSA, October 9, 1939.
92. Chicago *Defender,* January 6, 1940, p. 2; January 20, 1940, p. 6; January 27, 1940, p. 6; February 3, 1940, p. 8; February 17, 1940, p. 7; February 24, 1940, p. 8; March 2, 1940, p. 6; March 9, 1940, p. 7.
93. Ibid., January 6, 1940, p. 2.
94. Ibid., March 2, 1940, p. 6.
95. Ernest Palmer to MFSA, December 22, 1937.
96. Lee L. Bailey, May 16, 1986.
97. Chicago *Defender,* June 1, 1940, p. 5.
98. Ibid., September 7, 1940, p. 8.
99. *The Metropolitan Opening* (Chicago: Metropolitan Funeral System Association, September, 1940), pp. 1–2.
100. *A Monument to Bronze America Souvenir Book, 1940* (Chicago: Metropolitan Funeral System Association, 1940), no pagination. This widely distributed pamphlet commemorated the opening of the company's new home office.

101. Chicago *Defender,* September 7, 1940, p. 8.
102. MFSA, *The Metropolitan Opening,* p. 1.
103. Minutes, Board Meeting, MFSA, September 2, 1938.
104. Minutes, General Meeting, MFSA, January 21, 1946.
105. Ibid.
106. Chicago *Defender,* December 12, 1942, pp. 1, 4.
107. Ibid.
108. Ibid., March 24, 1944, p. 12.
109. Ibid., December 12, 1942, pp. 1, 4.
110. Minutes, Board Meeting, MFSA, July 6, 1943.
111. Chicago Metropolitan Mutual Assurance Company Executive Roster, 1960; "Chicago Metropolitan Mutual: A Negro Insurance Company Which Is Doing Big Business," *Our World,* 7 (January 1952), p. 55.
112. Minutes, Board Meeting, MFSA, April 30, 1945.
113. Minutes, Board Meeting, MFSA, May 23, 1945.
114. Mrs. Dorothy Harper, December 4, 1985.
115. Minutes, General Meeting, MFSA, January 17, 1944.
116. Minutes, General Meeting, MFSA, January 21, 1946.
117. MFSA to Illinois Department of Insurance, September 30, 1946.
118. Ibid.

2. The Metropolitan Mutual Assurance Company of Chicago, 1947–1952

1. Interview, Jesse L. Moman, March 6, 1986.
2. Interview, Baker Cole, February 26, 1986. Mr. Cole is the nephew of Robert A. Cole. Baker Cole worked with the company from 1937–1978.
3. Minutes, Board Meeting, Metropolitan Mutual Assurance Company of Chicago, November 25, 1946.
4. Chicago Metropolitan Mutual Assurance Company Executive Roster, 1960.
5. Illinois Department of Insurance Examination of the MMACC, June 24, 1947, p. 4.
6. Alzater Timmons to Robert E. Weems, Jr., October 27, 1986. Mrs. Timmons, now retired, formerly served as Chicago Metropolitan's personnel manager. She provided information concerning Leo Blackburn from her files.
7. Interview, Lee L. Bailey, October 21, 1986.
8. Illinois Department of Insurance Examination of the MMACC, June 24, 1947, p. 3.
9. Illinois Department of Insurance Examination of the MMACC, October 30, 1953, pp. 5, 7.
10. Interview, Robert F. Jones, June 27, 1986.
11. Minutes, Board Meeting, MMACC, September 2, 1947.
12. Chicago Metropolitan Mutual Assurance Company Executive Roster, 1960.
13. *CMMAC News and Views,* July 1956, p. 4. This publication served as the company newsletter during the 1950s.
14. Minutes, Board Meeting, MMACC, September 22, 1947.
15. Minutes, Board Meeting, MMACC, January 15, 1951.
16. Chicago Metropolitan Mutual Assurance Company Executive Roster, 1960.
17. Company pamphlet, "Metropolitan Mutual Assurance Company," 1950, no pagination; Jesse L. Moman, September 24, 1985; Robert F. Jones, June 27, 1986.
18. Jesse L. Moman, September 24, 1985; Lee L. Bailey, May 16, 1986.
19. Robert A. Cole to N. P. Parkinson, director of the Illinois Department of Insurance, October 5, 1948.

20. N. P. Parkinson to MMACC, October 13, 1948.

21. Minutes, Board Meeting, MMACC, November 15, 1948.

22. Minutes, Annual Meeting, MMACC, January 15, 1951; Minutes, Board Meeting, MMACC, January 28, 1952. Retirees with at least twenty years of service by the age of sixty-five were to receive monthly pensions of seventy-five dollars. Those with less than twenty years of service at age 65 received a proportionately reduced pension.

23. Interview, Donnie Jones, April 1, 1986. Mr. Jones, currently retired, began working with the company in 1940.

24. Ibid.

25. Ibid.

26. Molly Moon to Claude A. Barnett, January 11, 1951, Claude A. Barnett Papers, Chicago Historical Society.

27. Claude A. Barnett to Robert A. Cole, January 20, 1951, Claude A. Barnett Papers.

28. Molly Moon to Claude A. Barnett, March 3, 1951, Claude A. Barnett Papers.

29. Minutes, Board Meeting, MMACC, June 27, 1949.

30. Minutes, Board Meeting, MMACC, January 9, 1950.

31. Complaint against the MMACC filed by the Metropolitan Life Insurance Company, Case #51C-66, United States District Court for the Northern District of Illinois/Eastern Division, United States National Archives, Chicago, Illinois, pp. 3–4.

32. Ibid.

33. MMACC response to the January 12, 1951, complaint filed by the Metropolitan Life Insurance Company, ibid.

34. Chicago *Defender,* January 20, 1951, p. 1.

35. William J. Trent, Jr., "Development of Negro Life Insurance Enterprises," M.A. thesis, University of Pennsylvania, 1932, p. 24.

36. Ibid., p. 25.

37. Frederick L. Hoffman, *Race Traits and the Tendencies of the American Negro* (New York: Macmillan, 1896), pp. 328–29.

38. Harry H. Pace, "The Attitude of Life Insurance Companies toward Negroes," *Southern Workman,* 57 (1928), p. 4.

39. Ibid.

40. Marquis James, *The Metropolitan Life: A Study in Business Growth* (New York: Viking, 1947), pp. 338–39.

41. Pace, "Life Insurance Companies and Negroes," p. 3; Chicago *Whip,* July 27, 1929, p. 1.

42. Ibid., p. 7.

43. Associated Negro Press, news release, October 2, 1944, Claude A. Barnett Papers.

44. For specific instances see Chicago *Whip,* July 27, 1929, pp. 1, 4; Pace, "Life Insurance Companies and Negroes," p. 6.

45. Chicago *Courier,* July 7, 1951, p. 5.

46. Associated Negro Press, news release, January 25, 1951, Claude A. Barnett Papers.

47. Chicago *Defender,* March 31, 1951, p. 13.

48. Chicago *Courier,* July 7, 1951, p. 5.

49. Consent Decree, November 7, 1952, Case #51C-66, *Metropolitan Life vs. Metropolitan Mutual,* United States National Archives, Chicago, Illinois.

50. Minutes, Annual Meeting, MMACC, January 19, 1953.

51. Chicago *Defender,* July 19, 1952, pp. 1–2.

52. Minutes, Annual Meeting, MMACC, January 19, 1953.

53. *A Brief History of the Chicago Metropolitan Mutual Assurance Company*, (Chicago: CMMAC Public Relations Department, 1977), p. 8.

54. *A Dream Come True: The Story of the MMAC, 1927–1952* (Chicago: MMACC, 1952), no pagination.

55. Chicago *Defender*, January 3, 1953, pp. 1, 4.

56. Ibid.

3. The Chicago Metropolitan Mutual Assurance Company, 1953–1957

1. Minutes, Board Meeting, Chicago Metropolitan Mutual Assurance Company, March 16, 1953.

2. Minutes, Board Meeting, CMMAC, April 13, 1953.

3. Minutes, Board Meeting, CMMAC, April 5, 1954.

4. Minutes, Annual Meeting, CMMAC, January 17, 1955.

5. Ibid.

6. Interview, Lynn Langston, Jr., August 21, 1986.

7. Ibid.

8. Interview, Jesse Moman, February 11, 1986.

9. "Insurance Anniversary: Metropolitan Mutual of Chicago Marks 25th Year," *Ebony*, 8 (January 1953), p. 79.

10. Ibid., p. 82.

11. Robert A. Cole, "How I Made a Million," *Ebony*, 9 (September 1954), pp. 43–52.

12. Chicago *Tribune*, July 9, 1955, p. 8.

13. Chicago *Sun Times*, December 3, 1955, p. 1; Chicago *American*, December 4, 1955, pp. 1, 6; Associated Negro Press, news releases, December 12, 1955, December 14, 1955, Claude A. Barnett Papers, Chicago Historical Society.

14. Chicago *Defender*, March 8, 1941, p. 6; October 27, 1945, p. 3.

15. Ibid., September 27, 1941, p. 19.

16. Chicago *American*, December 4, 1955, p. 6; Associated Negro Press, news releases, December 12, 1955, December 14, 1955, Claude A. Barnett Papers. In December 1960, Mary F. Cole and Robert (Kelly) Rose were married.

17. Minutes, Annual Meeting, CMMAC, January 16, 1956; Board Meetings, January 16, 1956; February 6, 1956, March 19, 1956, April 16, 1956, April 30, 1956, June 18, 1956.

18. Minutes, Board Meeting, CMMAC, December 12, 1955.

19. Ibid.

20. Minutes, Annual Meeting, CMMAC, January 16, 1956.

21. Chicago Metropolitan Mutual Assurance Company Executive Roster, 1960.

22. Minutes, Board Meeting, CMMAC, January 16, 1956.

23. Ibid.

24. Chicago *Daily News*, March 12, 1957, pp. 1, 9.

25. Minutes, Board Meeting, CMMAC, January 16, 1956.

26. Associated Negro Press, news release, August 8, 1956, Claude A. Barnett Papers.

27. Minutes, Board Meeting, CMMAC, November 19, 1956.

28. Minutes, Board Meeting, CMMAC, April 3, 1957.

29. Minutes, Board Meeting, CMMAC, June 26, 1957.

30. Minutes, Annual Meeting, CMMAC, January 21, 1957.

31. Illinois Department of Insurance Examination of the Chicago Metropolitan Mutual Assurance Company, March 15, 1957, pp. 6–7.

32. Ibid.

33. Interviews, Leon Sanders, May 27, 1986. Mr. Sanders worked with the company from 1942 to 1975. Lieutenant R. Booker, July 17, 1986. Mr. Booker worked with the company from 1951 to 1975. Besides these two men, a consensus existed among other "old-timers" stating that Robert A. Cole would have settled the 1957 dispute through personal intervention, rather than permit it to develop into a full-scale strike.

34. Interview, Herbert Cooley, April 15, 1986. Mr. Cooley, now retired, worked in the company's Agency Department for more than 30 years.

35. Minutes, Board Meeting, CMMAC, August 6, 1957.

36. Minutes, Administrative Committee Meetings, CMMAC, July 11, 1957, July 31, 1957.

37. Company pamphlet, "Chicago Metropolitan Mutual Assurance Company: Teamwork," CMMAC, 1957, no pagination.

38. Herbert W. Cooley, April 15, 1986; Lynn L. Langston, August 21, 1986.

39. Chicago Metropolitan Mutual Assurance Company Executive Roster, 1960.

40. Lynn Langston, August 21, 1986; Jesse L. Moman, February 11, 1986.

41. Report from Lorenzo D. Jones to the CMMAC Board of Directors, November 22, 1957.

42. Ibid.

43. Ibid.

44. Ibid.

45. Minutes, Board Meeting, CMMAC, November 27, 1957.

46. Minutes, Annual Meeting, CMMAC, January 20, 1958.

4. The Chicago Metropolitan Mutual Assurance Company as an African American Community Institution, 1927–1957

1. Cayton and Drake, *Black Metropolis,* p. 395.

2. Mark Newman, "On the Air with Jack L. Cooper: The Beginnings of Black Appeal Radio," *Chicago History,* 12 (Summer 1983), pp. 51, 54–56.

3. *Bronzeman,* April 1932, p. 24.

4. Ibid.

5. Ibid.

6. Ibid., June 1931, pp. 7, 38.

7. Abby Arthur Johnson and Ronald Maberry Johnson, *Propaganda and Aesthetics: The Literary Politics of Afro-American Magazines in the Twentieth Century* (Amherst: University of Massachusetts Press, 1979), p. 109.

8. Ibid.

9. *Bronzeman,* June 1931, pp. 4–5.

10. Ibid.

11. Ibid.

12. *Bronzeman,* June 1931, pp. 9–11.

13. *Bronzeman,* May 1932, p. 6.

14. *Bronzeman,* May 1932, p. 6; June 1932, p. 23; July 1932, p. 30; August 1932, p. 22; September 1932, p. 29. The cities Andrews visited were: Indianapolis, Indiana; St. Louis, Missouri; Kansas City, Kansas; Oklahoma City, Oklahoma; Tulsa, Oklahoma; New Orleans, Louisiana; Dallas, Texas; San Antonio, Texas; Houston, Texas; Birmingham, Alabama; Memphis, Tennessee; Nashville, Tennessee; Louisville, Kentucky; and Cincinnati, Ohio.

15. Ibid.

16. Ibid., September 1932, p. 29.

17. Johnson and Johnson, *Propaganda and Aesthetics,* p. 109.
18. Ibid., pp. 109–10.
19. *Bronzeman,* July 1931, p. 6; August 1931, p. 6.
20. *Bronzeman,* July 1931, p. 7; September 1931, p. 5.
21. *Bronzeman,* August 1931, p. 35.
22. *Bronzeman,* April 1932, p. 35.
23. *Bronzeman,* November 1931, p. 4; April 1932, p. 35.
24. Robert A. Cole, "How I Made a Million," *Ebony,* 9 (September 1954), p. 50.
25. Donn Rogosin, *Invisible Men: Life in Baseball's Negro Leagues* (New York: Atheneum, 1983), p. 104.
26. Ibid., p. 105.
27. Robert Peterson, *Only the Ball Was White* (New York: McGraw-Hill, 1984; first published in 1970), pp. 92–93.
28. Rogosin, *Invisible Men,* p. 107.
29. Interview, Robert A. Cole, Jr., March 4, 1986. Mr. Cole is the adopted son of Robert A. Cole.
30. Peterson, *Only the Ball Was White,* p. 115.
31. Ibid., p. 114.
32. Ibid.
33. Chicago *Defender,* February 27, 1932, p. 8.
34. Illinois Writers Project, Negro in Illinois Series, MSS IWP 132, folder 1; Memorandum dated December 20, 1941, Vivian Harsh Collection, Carter G. Woodson Regional Library, Chicago, Illinois.
35. Chicago *Defender,* February 27, 1932, p. 8.
36. Ibid.
37. Chicago *Defender,* October 9, 1932, p. 10.
38. Peterson, *Only the Ball Was White,* p. 93.
39. Ibid.
40. Chicago *Defender,* August 22, 1942, p. 24.
41. Chicago *Defender,* November 2, 1935, p. 13.
42. Interview, Joseph Moody, April 3, 1986. Mr. Moody is Horace G. Hall's nephew. Mr. Hall (now deceased) could not grant me an interview because of illness.
43. Peterson, *Only the Ball Was White,* p. 93.
44. Frederick Robb, ed., *The Negro in Chicago, 1779–1929* (Chicago: Washington Intercollegiate Club of Chicago, 1929), p. 141; Allan H. Spear, *Black Chicago: The Making of a Negro Ghetto, 1890–1920* (Chicago: University of Chicago Press, 1967), p. 101.
45. Spear, *Black Chicago,* p. 100.
46. Robb, *The Negro in Chicago,* pp. 141–45.
47. Minutes, Board of Directors Meeting, Wabash Avenue YMCA, February 23, 1928, Wabash Avenue YMCA Collection, University of Illinois-Chicago.
48. Chicago *Defender,* September 28, 1935, p. 4.
49. Chicago *Defender,* November 9, 1935, p. 4.
50. Minutes, Board Meeting, Wabash Avenue YMCA, May 17, 1938.
51. Ibid., January 28, 1939; May 16, 1939.
52. Interview, Lee L. Bailey, August 3, 1987.
53. *Crisis,* 45 (January 1938), pp. 1, 5. While the *Crisis* stated that all MFSA employees were dues-paying members of the NAACP, Lee L. Bailey believes this may have been an overstatement. Although Robert A. Cole and Fred W. Lewing urged employees to become NAACP members, it was not mandatory. Whereas

most personnel complied with Cole's and Lewing's wishes, Bailey, who worked for the MFSA during this period, could not verify a 100 percent response.

54. Lee L. Bailey, August 3, 1987.

55. Charles R. Branham, "The Transformation of Black Political Leadership in Chicago: 1864–1942," Ph.D. dissertation, University of Chicago, 1981, pp. 272–73; Harold F. Gosnell, *Negro Politicians: The Rise of Negro Politics in Chicago* (Chicago: University of Chicago Press, 1935), p. 195; Associated Negro Press, news release, December 19, 1932, Claude A. Barnett Papers, Chicago Historical Society.

56. Such persons included: James B. Cashin, appointed civil service commissioner of the City of Chicago in 1942; Sidney P. Brown, who served on the Chicago Board of Education from 1945–1958; Melvin McNairy, elected to the Illinois House of Representatives in 1964; and Charles Chew, Jr., who served as both a Chicago alderman (1963–1967) and a member of the Illinois legislature from 1967 until his death in 1986.

57. Cayton and Drake, *Black Metropolis*, pp. 687–710.

58. Dempsey J. Travis, *An Autobiography of Black Jazz* (Chicago: Urban Research Institute, 1983), p. 86.

59. Ibid., pp. 86–88.

60. Ibid., pp. 36, 88–89. The Vincennes Hotel, located at 601 E. 36th Street, was the favorite meeting place of Bronzeville's elite from 1910 to 1940. Bacon's Casino, located at 49th and Wabash Avenue, was a converted garage that opened in 1940. When the Parkway Ballroom opened in 1940, the importance of the other facilities declined.

61. "Black Metropolis Historic District," proposal submitted to the Commission on Chicago Historical and Architectural Landmarks, March 7, 1984, pp. 1, 5.

62. Travis, *Black Jazz*, pp. 83–84, 93–110.

63. Ibid., p. 43.

64. Interview, Etta Moten-Barnett, December 8, 1985. Mrs. Moten-Barnett, the widow of Claude A. Barnett (the founder of the Associated Negro Press), was prestigious in her own right. She gained fame as a concert singer and actress. In 1942, she sang the lead in the Broadway production of *Porgy and Bess*. During her professional career, Mrs. Moten-Barnett had the opportunity to travel extensively. Consequently, her assertion that the Parkway Ballroom was the finest ballroom in America not associated with a hotel must be taken seriously.

65. Interview, Jesse L. Moman, September 24, 1985.

66. To determine the Parkway Ballroom's popularity, I interviewed several longtime black Chicago residents at the William L. Dawson Nursing Home on Chicago's South Side. The following individuals graciously assisted me: Willella Lomax, Fred Spencer, Curtis Flucker, Bertha McMillan (November 11, 1985); John Smith, Buelah Boyd, Emma Richmond (November 25, 1985); Vida Madison, Jerry Moses, Jr., Edwina Helm, Almetta Dooley (December 9, 1985); Beatrice Wright, Edward Watts, Annie Evans, Nancy Long (December, 30, 1985). On January 3, 1986, I interviewed my mother, Dolores Weems, herself a lifelong Chicago resident. I conducted another useful interview with Dr. Marjorie Stewart Joyner on May 28, 1986. Dr. Joyner, who recently died at the age of 98, lived at the same South Side location for over 75 years. Dr. Joyner, besides having served as a close associate with Dr. Mary McLeod Bethune for nearly fifty years, worked with Madame C. J. Walker (the cosmetics queen) and established a Chicago branch of Madame C. J. Walker Products at 47th and South Parkway.

67. Interview, Clarence M. Markham, Jr., February 19, 1986. Mr. Markham, along with four other railroad employees, established *The Negro Traveler and Conventioneer* because of their concern over the plight of black travelers during the 1930s and 1940s. If a black traveler during this period was unaware of a particular municipality's laws/customs relating to accommodations for blacks, or if the black traveler did not have relatives or friends in a particular locale, such African American travelers were often forced to sleep in railroad stations. *The Negro Traveler and Conventioneer* served as a national directory service for black travelers. Advertising revenue, secured from the black-owned hotels and restaurants that appeared in *The Negro Traveler and Conventioneer,* kept the magazine afloat.

68. "Insurance Anniversary: Metropolitan Mutual of Chicago Marks 25th Year," *Ebony,* (January 1953), p. 81.

69. Jesse L. Moman, September 24, 1985.

70. Clarence M. Markham, February 19, 1986.

71. Interview, Edward A. Trammell, October 9, 1985. Mr. Trammell joined Metropolitan Mutual as an agent in 1951 and spent more than thirty years with the company.

72. Ibid.

73. Jesse L. Moman, March 5, 1986.

74. Edward A. Trammell, October 9, 1985; Jesse L. Moman, September 24, 1985. Ironically, John Seder and Berkeley Burrell's 1971 study, *Getting It Together: Black Businessmen in America* (an essentially positive depiction of black economic development), contended that black institutions such as the Parkway Ballroom and Dining Room declined because desegregation offered black consumers an opportunity to escape their "captivity" to black businessmen. Implying that desegregation "freed" blacks from the oppressive grasp of black businessmen is ahistorical. Black businessmen neither created nor enforced America's segregation laws. See Seder and Burrell, p. 212.

75. Merah Steven Stuart, *An Economic Detour: A History of Insurance in the Lives of American Negroes* (College Park, MD: McGrath, 1969; originally published in 1940), p. xxi; National Insurance Association, 50th Anniversary Convention Program, July 20–23, 1970, Richmond, Virginia, pp. 10–13.

76. Chicago Negro Insurance Association, *Negro Insurance Week, 1947,* p. 3.

77. Ibid., p. 10.

78. Ibid., p. 14.

79. Jesse L. Moman, September 24, 1985.

5. The Chicago Metropolitan "Family," 1927–1957

1. Interview, Jesse Moman, September 24, 1985. Besides Mr. Moman, everyone who remembers the Cole administration verified the existence of a "family" atmosphere.

2. As in note 1, every person who remembers Mr. Cole noted his generous and gregarious nature.

3. Walter B. Weare, *Black Business in the New South: A Social History of the North Carolina Mutual Life Insurance Company* (Urbana: University of Illinois Press, 1973), pp. 139–40; Alexa Benson Henderson, *Atlanta Life Insurance Company: Guardian of Black Economic Dignity* (Tuscaloosa: University of Alabama Press, 1990), p. 126.

4. Charles E. Hall, *Negroes in the United States, 1920–1932* (Washington, DC: United States Bureau of the Census, 1935), pp. 496–98; *The Social and Economic*

Status of the Black Population in the United States: An Historical View, 1790–1978 (Washington, DC: United States Bureau of the Census, 1979), pp. 78–79; John Sibley Butler, *Entrepreneurship and Self-Help among Black Americans: A Reconsideration of Race and Economics* (Albany: SUNY Press, 1991), pp. 297, 309.

5. Joseph A. Pierce, *Negro Business and Business Education: Their Present and Prospective Development* (New York: Harper, 1947), p. 128; *Best's Life Insurance Reports, 1946 (41st Annual Edition)* (New York: Alfred M. Best, 1946), pp. 510, 575; *Best's Life Insurance Reports, 1991 (85th Annual Edition)*, pp. 1499, 1998; *Black Enterprise*, 21 (June 1991), p. 172. At the end of 1945, the combined assets of the forty-four members of the National Negro Insurance Association was $69,874,946. By contrast, Metropolitan Life claimed $7,561,997,270 in admitted assets at the end of 1945; the Prudential Life Insurance Company listed $6,355,984,306. In 1990, the fifteen largest black insurance companies, according to *Black Enterprise*, had combined assets of $796 million. Met Life and Prudential claimed over $103 billion and $133 billion, respectively.

6. Interview, Lee L. Bailey, May 16, 1986.

7. Ibid.

8. Illinois Department of Insurance Examination of the MFSA, November 24, 1931, pp. 6–7.

9. Lee L. Bailey, May 16, 1986.

10. Ibid.

11. Ibid.

12. Ibid.

13. Minutes, Annual Meeting, Metropolitan Funeral System Association, January 15, 1934.

14. Minutes, Annual Meeting, MFSA, January 16, 1939.

15. Associated Negro Press, news release, December 19, 1932, Claude A. Barnett Papers, Chicago Historical Society.

16. Minutes, Board Meeting, MFSA, December 29, 1927.

17. Illinois Department of Insurance Examination of the MFSA, November 24, 1931, p. 3.

18. Ibid.

19. Illinois Department of Insurance Examination of the MFSA, June 10, 1932.

20. Ibid., pp. 2–3.

21. Ibid., Conclusion.

22. Associated Negro Press, news release, December 19, 1932, Claude A. Barnett Papers.

23. Minutes, Annual Meeting, MFSA, January 15, 1934.

24. *A Place in the Sun: A Pictorial and Graphic Review of the Rise of the Metropolitan Funeral System Association* (Chicago: MFSA, 1930), no pagination; obituary, Rev. Mansfield Edward Bryant Peck, May 20, 1946.

25. Minutes, Annual Meetings, MFSA, January 15, 1934, January 21, 1935.

26. Lee L. Bailey, May 16, 1986.

27. Cayton and Drake, *Black Metropolis*, p. 223.

28. Interview, Dorothy Harper (Fred Lewing's daughter), December 4, 1985.

29. Interview, Donnie Jones, April 1, 1986.

30. Chicago *Defender*, September 7, 1940, p. 8.

31. *A Monument to Bronze America: Souvenir Book* (Chicago: MFSA, 1940), p. 5.

32. Robert F. Jones, June 27, 1986; Jesse L. Moman, September 24, 1985.

33. Company pamphlet, "Metropolitan Mutual Assurance Company," 1950, no pagination.

34. Ibid.

35. Interview, Louise Wood, April 22, 1986. Mrs. Wood joined the company in 1947. She was also the daughter-in-law of Rosalee Wood.

36. Jesse L. Moman, September 2, 1985.

37. Ibid.

38. Ibid.

39. Interviews, Bowen Heffner, May 16, 1986; Lieutenant R. Booker, July 17, 1986; Robert Wilson, August 14, 1986. Mr. Heffner joined the company as an agent in 1942. He retired in 1981 as director of field operations and a board member. Mr. Booker used the flexible work schedule to become a noted black Chicago Boy Scout master. Mr. Wilson used the flexible work schedule to pursue an insurance broker's license. Besides developing into one of the company's most productive agents, Robert Wilson created a thriving insurance brokerage firm.

40. Alzater Timmons, April 3, 1986.

41. Ibid.

42. Louise Wood, April 22, 1986.

43. Edward A. Trammell II, October 9, 1985.

44. Ibid.

45. Interview, Cleland Brewer, April 14, 1986. Mr. Brewer, now retired, served in a variety of capacities in the Agency Department. Brewer informed the author that before joining the company in 1959, he was always impressed with CMMAC agents' "style."

46. Minutes, Annual Meeting, Metropolitan Mutual Assurance Company of Chicago, January 15, 1951; Board Meeting, January 28, 1952.

47. Lee L. Bailey, May 16, 1986.

48. Ibid.

49. Interview, Leon Sanders, May 26, 1986. Mr. Sanders joined the company as an agent in 1942.

50. Ibid.

51. Ibid. Besides Mr. Sanders, the vast majority of persons who remember Robert A. Cole noted his fairness.

52. Lee L. Bailey, May 16, 1986.

53. Chicago *Defender,* February 5, 1944, p. 13.

54. Illinois Department of Insurance Examination of CMMAC, March 15, 1957, Introduction.

55. Jesse L. Moman, March 13, 1986.

56. Ibid.

57. Minutes, Board Meeting, CMMAC, October 15, 1956.

58. *Best's Life Insurance Reports, 1955–1956* (New York: Alfred M. Best, 1955), p. 214; *Best's Reports, 1959–1960* (New York: Alfred M. Best, 1959), p. 337.

59. Illinois Department of Insurance Examination of CMMAC, March 15, 1957, pp. 6–7; Minutes, Annual Meeting, CMMAC, January 21, 1957.

60. Illinois Department of Insurance Examination of CMMAC, March 15, 1957, pp. 6–7.

61. Herbert W. Cooley, April 15, 1986.

62. Interviews, Jesse L. Moman, February 11, 1986; Donnie Jones, April 1, 1986; James Isbell, May 27, 1986. Mr. Isbell joined CMMAC in 1956 after a distinguished tenure at Chicago's Jackson Mutual. See chapter 6 for a discussion of Isbell's activities at CMMAC.

63. Edward A. Trammell II, February 4, 1986.

64. Jesse L. Moman, February 11, 1986.

65. Ibid.

66. Interviews, Robert Wilson, August 14, 1986; Albertha Bankhead, April 15, 1986. Mrs. Bankhead joined the company in 1954.

67. Albertha Bankhead, April 15, 1986.

68. Interviews, Jesse L. Moman, February 11, 1986; Herbert W. Cooley, April 15, 1986; Leon Sanders, May 27, 1986; Lynn Langston, Jr., August 21, 1986.

6. Chicago Metropolitan, 1958–1985

1. Edward Franklin Frazier, "Human, All Too Human: How Some Negroes Have Developed Vested Interests in the System of Racial Segregation," *Survey Graphic*, 36 (January 1947), p. 75.

2. Minutes, Annual Meeting, Chicago Metropolitan Mutual Assurance Company, January 20, 1958.

3. Minutes, Annual Meeting, CMMAC, January 19, 1959.

4. Minutes, Agency Committee Meeting, CMMAC, February 20, 1958; Board Meeting, January 26, 1958.

5. Minutes, Agency Committee Meeting, CMMAC, February 20, 1958; Board Meeting, April 22, 1959.

6. M. W. Newman, "Jobs Begging for Thousands of Trained Negroes," Chicago *Daily News*, March 12, 1957, pp. 1, 10.

7. Interview, James S. Isbell, May 27, 1986.

8. Harry H. Pace, "The Attitude of Life Insurance Companies toward Negroes," *Southern Workman*, 57 (1928), pp. 4–5.

9. Interviews, Herbert W. Cooley, April 15, 1986; Lynn Langston, Jr., August 21, 1986; John E. Fitzpatrick, April 17, 1986.

10. Interview, Weathers Y. Sykes, April 15, 1986.

11. James S. Isbell, May 27, 1986; Cleland Brewer, April 16, 1986; Lynn Langston, Jr., August 21, 1986.

12. Report from Lorenzo D. Jones to CMMAC Board of Directors, November 22, 1957.

13. Cleland Brewer, April 16, 1986.

14. Ibid.

15. Minutes, Board Meeting, CMMAC, November 22, 1961.

16. Jesse L. Moman, February 11, 1986.

17. Ibid.

18. *Pilot*, 11 (post-convention issue, 1963), pp. 4–5. The *Pilot* is the National Insurance Association's official publication.

19. *Pilot*, 16 (August 1967), p. 3.

20. Minutes, Annual Meeting, CMMAC, January 21, 1963; Board Meeting, February 27, 1963.

21. Minutes, Annual Meeting, CMMAC, January 20, 1964.

22. Minutes, Annual Meeting, CMMAC, January 18, 1965.

23. Ibid.

24. Minutes, Board Meeting, CMMAC, September 10, 1965.

25. Ibid.

26. Minutes, Annual Meeting, CMMAC, January 17, 1966.

27. Weathers Y. Sykes, April 15, 1986.

28. Weathers Y. Sykes, April 15, 1986; Jesse L. Moman, February 11, 1986; Cleland Brewer, April 16, 1986.

29. *Pilot*, 16 (August 1967), p. 3.

30. Minutes, Annual Meeting, CMMAC, January 16, 1967.

31. Minutes, Board Meeting, CMMAC, January 24, 1967.

32. Minutes, Annual Meeting, CMMAC, January 15, 1968.

33. Minutes, Board Meeting, CMMAC, January 31, 1968.

34. Minutes, Board Meeting, CMMAC, May 22, 1968.

35. Minutes, Annual Meeting, CMMAC, January 19, 1970.

36. Minutes, Board Meeting, CMMAC, January 20, 1965.

37. Ernest R. Rather, ed., *Chicago Negro Almanac and Reference Book* (Chicago: Chicago Negro Almanac Publishing Company, 1972), p. 75.

38. Minutes, Board Meeting, CMMAC, January 27, 1960.

39. Minutes, Board Meetings, CMMAC, January 27, 1960; January 17, 1961.

40. Minutes, Annual Meeting, CMMAC, January 18, 1965.

41. Minutes, Annual Meeting, CMMAC, January 17, 1966.

42. Ibid.

43. Minutes, Annual Meeting, CMMAC, January 15, 1968.

44. Minutes, Board Meeting, CMMAC, January 28, 1969.

45. Minutes, Annual Meeting, CMMAC, January 19, 1970; Board Meeting, February 3, 1970.

46. James S. Isbell, May 27, 1986.

47. Minutes, Executive Committee Meeting, CMMAC, February 11, 1971.

48. Minutes, Annual Meeting, CMMAC, January 17, 1972.

49. Minutes, Board Meeting, CMMAC, December 20, 1972. The majority of group insurance agreements secured by CMMAC were reinsurance pacts. Several major corporations, in an attempt to assist black business development, provided black insurers a portion of their group insurance needs. Ironically, Metropolitan Life, which attempted to destroy CMMAC during the early 1950s, ceded Chicago Met millions of dollars of its group insurance coverage during the 1970s. See *Pilot,* October 1975, p. 2.

50. Minutes, Board Meetings, CMMAC, December 20, 1972; January 28, 1973.

51. Rumor Oden, July 9, 1986.

52. James S. Isbell, May 27, 1986.

53. Ibid.

54. Minutes, Annual Meeting, CMMAC, January 20, 1975.

55. Minutes, Board Meeting, CMMAC, March 12, 1975.

56. Minutes, Board Meeting, CMMAC, March 20, 1975.

57. Minutes, Executive Committee Meeting, CMMAC, March 27, 1975.

58. Minutes, Board Meeting, CMMAC, September 22, 1976.

59. Weathers Y. Sykes, April 15, 1986.

60. Minutes, Executive Committee Meeting, CMMAC, September 1, 1976.

61. *A Brief History of the Chicago Metropolitan Mutual Assurance Company* (Chicago: CMMAC Public Relations Department, 1977). This booklet commemorated the company's fiftieth anniversary.

62. Minutes, Annual Meeting, CMMAC, January 17, 1977.

63. Minutes, Executive Committee Meeting, CMMAC, March 14, 1977.

64. Memorandum, Peter M. Cohen to Weathers Y. Sykes, July 11, 1977. Mr. Cohen represented the interior decorating firm of Richmond, Manhoff, and Marsh.

65. Louise Wood, April 22, 1986; Edward A. Trammell II, February 4, 1986; Joseph Moody, April 13, 1986; Jesse L. Moman, February 11, 1986.

66. Memorandum, Weathers Y. Sykes to Anderson M. Schweich, December 14, 1977.

67. Weathers Y. Sykes, April 15, 1986.

68. Ibid.

69. Bowen M. Heffner, May 14, 1986.

70. Lynn Langston, Jr., August 21, 1986; Robert Wilson, August 14, 1986.

71. *Pilot*, 18 (April 1969), p. 2.

72. *CMMAC*, July 1983, p. 1. The name of Chicago Metropolitan's in-house publication has changed several times. When it began during the 1950s, it was called *CMMAC News and Views*. During the early 1960s, the name changed to *Urban Life*. By the early 1970s, it assumed the name *Chicago Met Salesman*. Since then it has been known as *The Challenger, Magnum Force,* and *CMMAC*.

73. Josephine King, April 24, 1986; Minutes, Annual Meeting, CMMAC, January 18, 1982.

74. Josephine King, April 24, 1986.

75. Todd Jackson, April 15, 1986. Mr. Jackson, himself an FLMI, informed the author about this procedure. Besides King and Jackson, other CMMAC personnel who have earned FLMI status include Clinton E. Ward, Jr., Albert Halfacre, Maxine Harmon, and Joseph Moody.

76. Minutes, Executive Committee Meeting, CMMAC, January 25, 1980.

77. Minutes, Board Meeting, CMMAC, January 25, 1980.

78. *CMMAC*, June 1980, p. 1.

79. Minutes, Annual Meeting, CMMAC, January 21, 1980; Minutes, Annual Meeting, CMMAC, January 18, 1982.

80. Minutes, Nominating Committee Meeting, CMMAC, November 29, 1979.

81. Josephine King, April 24, 1986.

82. Rather than list each person individually, suffice it to say that a sizable number of informants claimed the company "family" appeared to dissipate during the 1970s.

83. Minutes, Annual Meeting, CMMAC, January 19, 1981.

84. Press release, Chicago Economic Development Commission, May 1, 1981.

85. Rumor L. Oden, July 9, 1986.

86. *Best's Review: Life/Health Insurance Edition,* 80 (August 1979), p. 35; 81 (August 1980), p. 39; 82 (September 1981), p. 71; 83 (September 1982), p. 44; 84 (August 1983), p. 46; 85 (July 1984), p. 76; 86 (July 1985), p. 66; 87 (July 1986), p. 25.

87. Ibid., 80 (August 1979), pp. 36–38; 81 (August 1980), pp. 40–42; 82 (September 1981), pp. 72–74; 83 (September 1982), pp. 45–47; 84 (August 1983), pp. 46–49; 85 (July 1984), pp. 77–79; 86 (July 1985), pp. 67–69; 87 (July 1986), pp. 26–28.

88. Ibid., 86 (July 1985), pp. 66–69; 87 (July 1986), pp. 25–28.

89. Norris L. Connally, "Black Insurance Companies," in *Proceedings of the National Black Economic Development Summit,* October 29, 1979, Baltimore, Maryland.

90. "Insurance that Preys on the Poor," *Consumer Reports,* 43 (November 1978), pp. 658–61.

91. *Consumer Reports,* 43 (November 1978), p. 661.

92. *Home Service Life Insurance: A Commentary,* National Association of Insurance Commissioners, December 1982, p. 93.

93. *Consumer Reports,* 43 (November 1978), p. 659.

94. Marjorie Stewart Joyner, May 28, 1986. Mrs. Joyner, who recently died at the age of 98, purchased an MFSA burial policy during the early 1930s. She informed the author that by the 1960s the money she paid in premiums exceeded the policy's $250 cash value. She also asserted that several of her elderly associates had similar experiences with industrial burial policies.

95. Lucius Millender, "Chicago Metropolitan Gets a New Lease on Life," *Black Enterprise*, 15 (June 1985), p. 164.
96. Minutes, Executive Committee Meeting, CMMAC, September 16, 1980.
97. Minutes, Board Meeting, CMMAC, December 15, 1982.
98. Robert Wilson, August 14, 1986; Lynn Langston, Jr., August 21, 1986.
99. Robert Wilson, August 14, 1986.
100. *CMMAC*, December 1985, p. 1; Lynn Langston, Jr., August 21, 1986.

7. Epilogue

1. Proxy Statement, Special Policyholders Meeting, Chicago Metropolitan Mutual Assurance Company, November 9, 1990.
2. *Best's Insurance Reports: 81st Annual Edition* (Oldwick, NJ: A. M. Best, 1986), p. 535; *Best's 84th Annual Edition* (1989), p. 507.
3. *Best's Insurance Reports: 85th Annual Edition* (Oldwick, NJ: A. M. Best, 1990), p. 497.
4. Andrew Hacker, *Two Nations: Black and White, Separate, Hostile, Unequal* (New York: Ballantine, 1992), p. 102.
5. "1990 Census of Population and Housing Summary, Tape File 3A, Chicago, Illinois," Southern Illinois University at Edwardsville, Regional Research and Development Services.
6. Ibid.
7. *Best's 85th Annual Edition* (1990), p. 497.
8. Henderson, *Atlanta Life,* see chapters 1–4.
9. Ibid., pp. 46, 55, 60.
10. Shawn Kennedy, "A Change in Policy" (insurance overview), *Black Enterprise,* 16 (June 1986), pp. 175–76; Christopher C. Williams and Maynard Eaton, "Can Atlanta Life Be King of the Hill?" *Black Enterprise,* 18 (June 1988), pp. 251–54.
11. Josephine King to Robert E. Weems, Jr., July 6, 1993.
12. Proxy Statement, CMMAC Special Policyholders Meeting, November 9, 1990.
13. *Best's Insurance Reports: 81st Annual Edition* (Oldwick, NJ: A. M. Best, 1986), p. 2408.
14. Ibid., p. 2407.
15. "Holding On for Future Growth" (overview of African American financial institutions), *Black Enterprise,* 22 (June 1992), p. 174.
16. Ibid.
17. Ibid.
18. "Fortify or Die" (insurance overview), *Black Enterprise,* 19 (June 1989), p. 285.
19. Roger Barnes, "Shotgun Mergers" (insurance overview) *Black Enterprise,* 20 (June 1990), p. 205.
20. "A New Day for Black Financial Institutions?" (overview of African American financial institutions), *Black Enterprise,* 23 (June 1993), p. 146.
21. Roland Alston, "North Carolina Mutual's Policy for Growth," *Black Enterprise,* 20 (June 1990), pp. 214–18.
22. Williams and Eaton, "Atlanta Life," *Black Enterprise,* 18 (June 1988), pp. 251–54.
23. Solomon J. Herbert, "Reaching for the Stars," *Black Enterprise,* 19 (June 1989), pp. 295–98.

BIBLIOGRAPHY

Manuscript Collections

Chicago Historical Society, Chicago, Illinois
    Claude A. Barnett Papers
University of Chicago, Chicago, Illinois
    Julius W. Rosenwald Papers
University of Illinois-Chicago, Chicago, Illinois
    Chicago Urban League Papers
    Wabash Avenue YMCA Papers
Vivian Harsh African American History Collection, Carter G. Woodson
    Regional Library, Chicago, Illinois
    Negro in Illinois Series

Government Documents

Case #51C-66, *Metropolitan Life Insurance Company vs. Metropolitan Mutual Assurance Company of Chicago,* United States District Court for the Northern District of Illinois/Eastern Division, United States National Archives, Chicago, Illinois.
Illinois Department of Insurance Examinations of the Metropolitan Funeral System Association, the Metropolitan Mutual Assurance Company of Chicago, and the Chicago Metropolitan Mutual Assurance Company: November 24, 1931; June 10, 1932; December 7, 1933; July 10, 1935; December 22, 1937; January 22, 1940; July 30, 1941; October 1, 1943; June 24, 1947; March 1, 1950; October 30, 1953; March 15, 1957. Chicago Metropolitan Assurance Company Archives, Chicago, Illinois.

Chicago Metropolitan Assurance Company Documents/Publications

A Brief History of the Chicago Metropolitan Mutual Assurance Company, 1977.
A Dream Come True: The Story of the Metropolitan Mutual Assurance Company, 1927–1952, 1952.
A Monument to Bronze America: Souvenir Book, 1940, 1940.
A Pictorial and Graphic Review of the Rise of the Metropolitan Funeral System Association and the Metropolitan Funeral Parlors, 1930.
CMMAC, June 1980; September 1980; January 1983; July 1983; May 1984; July 1984; August 1984; August 1985; December 1985.
CMMAC News and Views, May 1955; July 1956; August 1956.
Chicago Metropolitan Mutual Assurance Company Executive Roster, 1960.
Chicago Metropolitan Mutual Assurance Company: Teamwork, 1957.
Death Records, Metropolitan Funeral System Association, August 29, 1926–December 11, 1928.
Metropolitan Mutual Assurance Company, 1950.
Minutes of Board of Directors Meetings, Annual Meetings, Various Committee Meetings, 1927–1990.
Urban Life, May 1964; First Quarter, 1965.

Interviews

Bailey, Lee L. May 16, 1986; May 23, 1986; Chicago, Illinois.
Bankhead, Albertha. April 15, 1986, Chicago, Illinois.
Booker, Lieutenant R. July, 17, 1986, Chicago, Illinois.
Boyd, Buelah. November 11, 1985, Chicago, Illinois.
Boyd, Kathryn. December 9, 1985, Chicago, Illinois.
Brewer, Cleland. April 16, 1986, Chicago, Illinois.
Cole, Baker. February 26, 1986, Chicago, Illinois.
Cole, Robert A., Jr. March 4, 1986, Chicago, Illinois.
Cooley, Herbert W. April 15, 1986, Chicago, Illinois.
Dominguez, Velma. January 21, 1986, Chicago, Illinois.
Dooley, Almetta. December 9, 1985, Chicago, Illinois.
Evans, Anna. December 30, 1985, Chicago, Illinois.
Fitzpatrick, John E. April 17, 1986, Chicago, Illinois.
Fletcher, Camora. April 15, 1986, Chicago, Illinois.
Flucker, Curtis. November 11, 1985, Chicago, Illinois.
Grantham, James D. October 9, 1985; February 4, 1986; Chicago, Illinois.
Harper, Dorothy. December 4, 1985, Chicago, Illinois.
Hart, Vivian. December 9, 1985, Chicago, Illinois.
Heffner, Bowen M. May 14, 1986, Chicago, Illinois.
Helm, Edwina. December 9, 1985, Chicago, Illinois.
Hoggans, Bessie. December 9, 1985, Chicago, Illinois.
Isbell, James S. May 27, 1986, Chicago, Illinois.
Jackson, Jack. November 25, 1985, Chicago, Illinois.
Jones, Donnie. April 1, 1986, Chicago, Illinois.
Jones, Robert F. June 27, 1986, Chicago, Illinois.
Joyner, Marjorie Stewart. May 28, 1986, Chicago, Illinois.
King, Josephine. April 24, 1986, Chicago, Illinois.
Langston, Lynn, Jr. August 21, 1986, Chicago, Illinois.
Lomax, Willella. November 11, 1985, Chicago, Illinois.
Long, Nancy. December 30, 1985, Chicago, Illinois.
Madison, Vida. December 9, 1985, Chicago, Illinois.
Markham, Clarence, Jr. February 19, 1986, Chicago, Illinois.
McMillan, Bertha. November 11, 1985, Chicago, Illinois.
Moman, Jesse L. September 24, 1985; February 11, 1986; March 6, 1986; Chicago, Illinois.
Moody, Joseph. April 3, 1986, Chicago, Illinois.
Moten-Barnett, Etta. December 8, 1985, Chicago, Illinois.
Oden, Rumor L. July 9, 1986, Chicago, Illinois.
Richmond, Emma. November 23, 1985, Chicago, Illinois.
Sanders, Leon. May 27, 1986, Chicago, Illinois.
Smith, John. November 25, 1985, Chicago, Illinois.
Spencer, Fred. November 25, 1985, Chicago, Illinois.
Sykes, Weathers Y. April 15, 1986, Chicago, Illinois.
Timmons, Alzater. April 3, 1986, Chicago, Illinois.
Trammell, Edward A. II. October 9, 1985; February 4, 1986; Chicago, Illinois.
Watts, Edward. December 30, 1985, Chicago, Illinois.
Weems, Dolores. January 3, 1986, Chicago, Illinois.
Wilson, Robert. August 14, 1986, Chicago, Illinois.
Wood, Louise. April 22, 1986, Chicago, Illinois.

Wright, Beatrice. December 30, 1985, Chicago, Illinois.
Young, Jerry M., Jr. December 9, 1985, Chicago, Illinois.

Directories

Black, Ford S. *Black's Blue Book, 1917,* Chicago: Self-published, 1917.
Black, Ford S. *Black's Blue Book, 1921,* Chicago: Self-published, 1921.
Lakeside Directory of Chicago, 1917, volume I, Chicago: Chicago Directory Company, 1917.
Negro Neighborhood Business and Professional Directory, 1953, Chicago: Negro Neighborhood Business and Professional Directory, 1953.
Negro Neighborhood Business and Professional Directory, 1956, Chicago: Negro Neighborhood Business and Professional Directory, 1956.
Polk's Directory of Chicago, 1923, Volume II, Chicago: Polk & Company, 1923.
Polk's Directory of Chicago, 1928–1929, Chicago: Polk & Company, 1928.
Scott's Blue Book: A Classified Business and Service Directory of Greater Chicago's Colored Citizens' Commercial, Industrial, Professional, Religious, and Other Activities, 1947, Chicago: Scott's Business and Service Directory, 1947.
Scott's Blue Book: A Classified Business and Service Directory of Chicago's Citizens with Inter-Racial Features, 1956, Chicago: Scott's Business and Service Directory, 1956.
Scott's Blue Book Business and Service Directory: Chicago's Colored Citizens with Interracial Features, 1965, Momence, Ill: Scott's Blue Book, 1965.
Simms, James N. *Simms' Blue Book and National Negro Business and Professional Directory,* Chicago: Self-published, 1923.
South Side Business and Professional Review, 1936, Chicago: Five Hundred Men's Club, 1936.

Newspapers and Periodicals

Bronzeman
Chicago *American*
Chicago *Courier*
Chicago *Daily News*
Chicago *Defender*
Chicago *Sun-Times*
Chicago *Tribune*
New York *Times*

Books

Aptheker, Herbert. *The Negro People in America: A Critique of Gunnar Myrdal's "An American Dilemma."* Milwood, NY: Kraus, 1977. Originally published in 1946.
Bailey, Ronald W., ed. *Black Business Enterprise: Historical and Contemporary Perspectives.* New York: Basic, 1972.
Bates, Timothy M. *Black Capitalism: A Quantitative Analysis.* New York: Praeger, 1973.
Bracey, John H., August Meier, and Elliott Rudwick, eds. *Black Nationalism in America.* Indianapolis: Bobbs-Merrill, 1970.
Bryant, Keith L., Jr., and Henry C. Dethloff. *A History of American Business.* Englewood Cliffs, N.J.: Prentice-Hall, 1983.

Burrell, Berkeley G., and John Seder. *Getting It Together: Black Businessmen in America.* New York: Harcourt, Brace, Jovanovich, 1971.

Butler, John Sibley. *Entrepreneurship and Self-Help among Black Americans: A Reconsideration of Race and Economics.* Albany: State University of New York Press, 1991.

Cayton, Horace R., and St. Clair Drake. *Black Metropolis: A Study of Negro Life in a Northern City.* New York: Harcourt, Brace, 1970. Originally published in 1945.

Curry, Leonard P. *The Free Black in Urban America, 1800–1850.* Chicago: University of Chicago Press, 1981.

Daniel, Pete. *In the Shadow of Slavery: Peonage in the South, 1901–1969.* New York: Oxford University Press, 1972.

Davis, Malvin E. *Industrial Life Insurance in the United States.* New York: McGraw-Hill, 1944.

Du Bois, William Edward Burghardt. *Economic Cooperation among Negroes.* Atlanta: Atlanta University Press, 1907.

Essien-Udom, E. U. *Black Nationalism: A Search for Identity in America.* Chicago: University of Chicago Press, 1962.

Fletcher, Linda. *The Negro in the Insurance Industry.* Philadelphia: University of Pennsylvania Press, 1970.

Foner, Phillip S. *Organized Labor and the Black Worker, 1619–1973.* New York: International, 1976.

Franklin, John Hope, and Alfred A. Moss. *From Slavery to Freedom: A History of African-Americans,* seventh edition. New York: Knopf, 1994.

Frazier, Edward Franklin. *Black Bourgeoisie: The Rise of a New Middle Class in America.* New York: Collier, 1962. Originally published in 1957.

———. *The Negro Family in Chicago.* Chicago: University of Chicago Press, 1962.

Fredrickson, George M. *The Black Image in the White Mind: The Debate on Afro-American Character and Destiny, 1817–1914.* Middletown, Conn.: Wesleyan University Press, 1971.

Gloster, Jesse. *North Carolina Mutual Life Insurance Company: Its Historical Development and Current Operations.* New York: Arno, 1976.

Gosnell, Harold F. *Negro Politicians: The Rise of Negro Politics in Chicago.* Chicago: University of Chicago Press, 1935.

Grossman, James. *Land of Hope: Chicago, Black Southerners, and the Great Migration.* Chicago: University of Chicago Press, 1989.

Hacker, Andrew. *Two Nations: Black and White, Separate, Hostile, Unequal.* New York: Ballantine, 1992.

Hammurabi, F. H. *The Chicago Round Up, 1779–1951.* Chicago: House of Knowledge, 1951.

Harlan, Louis R. *Booker T. Washington: The Making of a Negro Leader, 1858–1901.* New York: Oxford University Press, 1972.

Harmon, J. H., Arnett G. Lindsay, and Carter G. Woodson. *The Negro as a Businessman.* College Park, Md.: McGrath, 1929.

Harris, Abram. *The Negro as Capitalist: A Study of Banking and Business.* Glouster, Mass.: Peter Smith, 1968. Originally published in 1936.

Henderson, Alexa B. *Atlanta Life Insurance Company: Guardian of Black Economic Dignity.* Tuscaloosa: University of Alabama Press, 1990.

Henderson, William L., and Larry C. Ledebur. *Economic Disparity: Problems and Strategies for Black America.* New York: Free Press, 1970.

Henri, Florette. *Black Migration: Movement North, 1900–1920.* Garden City, N.Y.: Anchor/Doubleday, 1975.

Higgs, Robert. *Competition and Coercion: Blacks in the American Economy, 1865–1914.* Cambridge: Cambridge University Press, 1977.

Hill, Robert A., ed. *The Marcus Garvey and Universal Negro Improvement Association Papers,* Volume I. Berkeley: University of California Press, 1983.

Hine, Darlene Clark, Elsa Barkley-Brown, and Rosalyn Tuborg-Penn, eds. *Black Women in America: An Historical Encyclopedia.* Brooklyn: Carlson, 1993.

Hirsch, Arnold R. *Making the Second Ghetto: Race and Housing in Chicago, 1940–1960.* New York: Cambridge University Press, 1983.

Hoffman, Frederick L. *Race Traits and Tendencies of the American Negro.* New York: Macmillan, 1896.

Holmes, S. J. *The Negro's Struggle for Survival: A Study in Human Ecology.* Berkeley: University of California Press, 1937.

Ijere, Martin O. *Survey of Afro-American Experience in the U.S. Economy.* Hicksville, N.Y.: Exposition, 1978.

James, Marquis. *The Metropolitan Life: A Study in Business Growth.* New York, Viking, 1947.

Johnson, Abby Arthur, and Ronald Maberry Johnson. *Propaganda and Aesthetics: The Literary Politics of Afro-American Magazines in the Twentieth Century.* Amherst: University of Massachusetts Press, 1979.

Keller, Morton. *The Life Insurance Enterprise, 1880–1910: A Study in the Limits of Corporate Power.* Cambridge: Harvard University Press, 1963.

Kennedy, Louise Venable. *The Negro Peasant Turns Cityward.* New York: AMS, 1968. Originally published in 1930.

Kinzer, Robert H., and Edward Sagarin. *The Negro in American Business: The Conflict between Separatism and Integration.* New York: Greenberg, 1950.

Kogan, Herman, and Lloyd Wendt. *Big Bill of Chicago.* Indianapolis: Bobbs-Merrill, 1953.

Lee, Roy F. *The Setting for Black Business Development: A Study in Sociology and Political Economy.* Ithaca, N.Y.: Cornell University School of Industrial and Labor Relations, 1973.

Light, Ivan H. *Ethnic Enterprise in America: Business and Welfare among Chinese, Japanese, and Blacks.* Berkeley: University of California Press, 1972.

McKelvey, Blake. *The Emergence of Metropolitan America, 1915–1966.* New Brunswick, N.J.: Rutgers University Press, 1968.

Mandle, Jay. *The Roots of Black Poverty.* Durham, N.C.: Duke University Press, 1978.

Marable, Manning. *How Capitalism Underdeveloped Black America.* Boston: South End, 1983.

Marks, Carole. *Farewell—We're Good and Gone: The Great Black Migration.* Bloomington: Indiana University Press, 1989.

Marshall, Robert A., and Eli A. Zubay. *The Debit System of Marketing Life and Health Insurance.* Englewood Cliffs, N.J.: Prentice-Hall, 1975.

Meier, August. *Negro Thought in America, 1880–1915.* Ann Arbor: University of Michigan Press, 1963.

Myrdal, Gunnar. *An American Dilemma: Twentieth Anniversary Edition.* New York: Harper & Row, 1962.

Oak, Vishnu V. *The Negro's Adventure in General Business.* Yellow Springs, Ohio: Antioch, 1949.

Ofari, Earl. *The Myth of Black Capitalism.* New York: Monthly Review, 1970.

Oladipupo, Raymond O. *How Distinct Is the Negro Market?* New York: Ogilvy & Mather, 1970.

Osthaus, Carl R. *Freedmen, Philanthropy, and Fraud: A History of the Freedmen's Savings Bank.* Urbana: University of Illinois Press, 1976.

Ottley, Roi. *New World A-Coming: Inside Black America.* Boston: Houghton Mifflin, 1943.

Peterson, Robert. *Only the Ball Was White.* New York: McGraw-Hill, 1984. Originally published in 1970.

Pierce, Joseph A. *Negro Business and Business Education: Their Present and Prospective Development.* New York: Harper, 1947.

Puth, Robert C. *Supreme Life: The History of a Negro Life Insurance Company.* New York: Arno, 1976.

Rapone, Anita. *The Guardian Life Insurance Company, 1860–1920: A History of a German-American Enterprise.* New York: New York University Press, 1987.

Robb, Frederick H., ed. *The Negro in Chicago, 1779–1929.* Chicago: Washington Intercollegiate Club of Chicago, 1929.

Rogosin, Donn. *Invisible Men: Life in Baseball's Negro Leagues.* New York: Atheneum, 1983.

Sherman, Richard B., ed. *The Negro and the City.* Englewood Cliffs, N.J.: Prentice-Hall, 1970.

Spear, Allan H. *Black Chicago: The Making of a Negro Ghetto, 1890–1920.* Chicago: University of Chicago Press, 1967.

Strickland, Arvarh. *History of the Chicago Urban League.* Urbana: University of Illinois Press, 1966.

Stuart, Merah Steven. *An Economic Detour: A History of Insurance in the Lives of American Negroes.* College Park, Md.: McGrath, 1969. Originally published in 1940.

Taitt, John, ed. *The Souvenir of Negro Progress: Chicago, 1779–1925.* Chicago: De Saible Association, 1925.

Thompson, Paul. *The Voice of the Past: Oral History.* New York: Oxford University Press, 1978.

Thorpe, Earl E. *The Mind of the Negro: An Intellectual History of Afro-Americans.* Westport, Conn.: Negro Universities Press, 1970. Originally published in 1961.

Travis, Dempsey J. *An Autobiography of Black Chicago.* Chicago: Urban Research Institute, 1981.

———. *An Autobiography of Black Jazz.* Chicago: Urban Research Institute, 1983.

Washington, Booker Taliafero. *The Negro in Business.* Boston: Hertel, Jenkins, 1907.

Weare, Walter B. *Black Business in the New South: A Social History of the North Carolina Mutual Life Insurance Company.* Urbana: University of Illinois Press, 1973.

Woodson, Carter G. *The Negro Professional Man and the Community.* New York: Negro Universities Press, 1969. Originally published in 1934.

Young, James O. *Black Writers of the Thirties.* Baton Rouge: Louisiana State University Press, 1973.

Articles

Bryson, Winfield. "Insurance Companies: An Overview," *Black Enterprise* 7 (June 1977): 121–27.

"Business in Bronzeville: Chicago, the Center of U.S. Negro Business," *Time* 31 (April 18, 1938): 70–71.

"Chicago Metropolitan Mutual: A Negro Insurance Company Which Is Doing Big Business," *Our World* 7 (January 1952): 54–56.

"Chicago: Money Capital of Negro America," *Our World* 6 (September 1951): 15–19.

"Chicago's R. A. Cole: He Bosses Funerals, Supports NAACP," *Crisis* 45 (January 1938): 1, 5.

Cole, Robert A. "How I Made a Million," *Ebony* 8 (September 1954): 43–52.

Foley, Eugene P. "The Negro Businessman: In Search of a Tradition," *Daedalus* 95 (1966): 107–44

Frazier, Edward Franklin. "Human, All Too Human: How Some Negroes Have Developed Vested Interests in the System of Racial Segregation," *Survey Graphic* 36 (January 1947): 74–75, 99–100.

Harris, Harrison L., Jr. "Negro Mortality in Chicago," *Social Service Review* 1 (1927): 58–60.

Hepburn, David. "Negro Americans' 100 Million Dollar Business," *Our World* 5 (May 1950): 16–22.

Holsey, Albion H. "Seventy-Five Years of Negro Business," *Crisis* 45 (July 1938): 201, 241–42.

"How Chicago Negroes Strike It Rich," *Color* 11 (March 1956): 22–33.

"Insurance Anniversary: Metropolitan Mutual of Chicago Marks 25th Year," *Ebony* 8 (January 1953): 79–82.

"Insurance-Leader in Negro Business," *Tuskegee Messenger* 3 (1927): 3.

"Insurance That Preys on the Poor," *Consumer Reports* 43 (November 1978): 658–61.

Jackson, James A. "Fraternal Societies Aid Race Progress," *Crisis* 45 (July 1938): 235–37, 244.

Lewis, Hylan G. "The Negro Business, Professional, and White Collar Worker," *Journal of Negro Education* 8 (1939): 430–45.

Millender, Lucius. "Chicago Metropolitan Gets a New Lease on Life," *Black Enterprise* 15 (June 1985): 163–66.

Newman, Mark. "On the Air with Jack L. Cooper: The Beginnings of Black Appeal Radio," *Chicago History* 12 (1983): 51–58.

Osthaus, Carl R. "The Rise and Fall of Jesse Binga, Black Financier," *Journal of Negro History* 58 (1973): 39–60.

Pace, Harry H. "The Attitude of Life Insurance Companies toward Negroes," *Southern Workman* 57 (January 1928): 3–7.

Pred, Allan. "Business Thoroughfares as Expressions of Urban Negro Culture," *Economic Geography* 39 (1963): 217–33.

Tucker, David. "Black Pride and Negro Business in the 1920s: George Washington Lee of Memphis," *Business History Review* 43 (1969): 435–51.

Woodson, Carter G. "Insurance Business among Negroes," *Journal of Negro History* 14 (1929): 202–26.

Monographs and Special Studies

"Black Metropolis Historic District." Preliminary Summary of Information Submitted to the Commission on Chicago Historical and Architectural Landmarks, March 7, 1984.

Bunche, Ralph J. "Conceptions and Ideologies of the Negro." Unpublished Research Memorandum, Carnegie-Myrdal Study of the Negro in America, 1940.

————. "The Programs, Ideologies, Tactics and Achievements of Negro Better-
    ment and Interracial Organizations." Unpublished Research Memoran-
    dum, Carnegie-Myrdal Study of the Negro in America, 1940.
Chicago Commission on Race Relations. *The Negro in Chicago: A Study of Race
    Relations and a Race Riot.* Chicago: University of Chicago Press, 1922.
Connally, Norris L. "Black Insurance Companies." Paper submitted at Second
    National Black Economic Development Summit, October 29, 1979, Balti-
    more, Maryland.
De A Reid, Ira. "The Negro in the American Economic System—Book I."
    Unpublished Research Memorandum, Carnegie-Myrdal Study of the
    Negro in America, 1940.
Drake, St. Clair. "The Negro Church and Voluntary Associations in Chicago."
    Unpublished Research Memorandum, Carnegie-Myrdal Study of the
    Negro in America, 1940.
"Factors in the Negro Market Influencing Attitudes toward Life Insurance."
    National Insurance Association, 1967.
Gannett, Henry. "Statistics of the Negroes in the United States." Occasional
    Paper Number 4, John F. Slater Fund, 1894.
Hall, Charles E. *Negroes in the United States, 1920–1932.* Washington, D.C.: United
    States Bureau of the Census, 1935.
Hauser, Philip, and Evelyn Kitagawa, eds. *Local Community Fact Book: Chicago
    Metropolitan Area, 1960.* Chicago: University of Chicago Press, 1963.
"Home Service Life Insurance: A Commentary." National Association of Insur-
    ance Commissioners, December 1962.
Johnson, Charles S. "Source Material for Patterns of Negro Segregation: Chi-
    cago, Illinois." Unpublished Research Memorandum, Carnegie-Myrdal
    Study of the Negro in America, 1940.
Johnson, Guion G., and Guy B. Johnson. "The Church and the Race Problem in
    the United States." Unpublished Research Memorandum, Carnegie-
    Myrdal Study of the Negro in America, 1940.
Palmer, E. N. "The Development of Negro Lodges in the United States."
    Unpublished Research Memorandum, Carnegie-Myrdal Study of the
    Negro in America, 1940.
"Problems and Opportunities Confronting Negroes in the Field of Business."
    Proceedings of National Conference on Small Business, Washington,
    D.C., November 30–December 2, 1961.
"Report on a Negro Health Survey and the Recommendations of the Advisory
    Committee to the Commissioner of Health." Chicago, 1927.
"The Negro in Business." Proceedings of the Fourth Conference for the Study of
    Negro Problems, Atlanta University, Atlanta, Georgia, May 30–31, 1899.
Woofter, T. J., Jr. "Summary and Recommendation on the Study of the Eco-
    nomic Status of the Negro." Unpublished Research Memorandum sub-
    mitted to the Julius Rosenwald Fund, 1930.

Theses and Dissertations

Branham, Charles. "The Transformation of Black Political Leadership in Chi-
    cago, 1864–1942." Ph.D. dissertation, University of Chicago, 1981.
Bryson, Winfield Octavus, Jr. "Negro Life Insurance Companies: A Comparative
    Analysis of the Operating and Financial Experience of Negro Legal
    Reserve Life Insurance Companies." Ph.D. dissertation, University of
    Pennsylvania, 1948.

Burrows, John H. "The Necessity of Myth: A History of the National Negro Business League, 1900–1945." Ph.D. dissertation, Auburn University, 1977.

Davis, Ralph. "Negro Newspapers in Chicago." M.A. thesis, University of Chicago, 1939.

De Mond, Albert L. "Certain Aspects of the Economic Development of the American Negro, 1865–1900." Ph.D. dissertation, Catholic University of America, 1945.

Spaulding, Norman W. "History of Black-Oriented Radio in Chicago, 1929–1963." Ph.D. dissertation, University of Illinois-Champaign/Urbana, 1981.

Trent, William J., Jr. "Development of Negro Life Insurance Enterprise." M.A. thesis, University of Pennsylvania, 1932.

Waite, Emerson E. "Social Factors in Negro Business Enterprise." M.A. thesis, Duke University, 1940.

Miscellaneous Materials

Best's Review: Life/Health Insurance Edition, 1977–1993.

Blackbook Business and Reference Guide, 1976. Chicago: National Publications Sales Agency, 1976.

Foster, A. L. *Chicago: City of Progress and Opportunity.* Chicago: Chicago Cosmopolitan Chamber of Commerce, 1957.

Metropolitan Funeral System Association, 1940 Report. Chicago: Dunne's Insurance Reports, 1940.

Metropolitan Mutual Assurance Company of Chicago, 1952. Chicago: Dunne's Insurance Reports, 1952.

National Insurance Association, 50th Annual Convention Program, Richmond, Virginia, July 20–23, 1970.

Negro Insurance Week, 1947. Chicago: Chicago Negro Insurance Association, 1947.

Negro Traveler and Conventioneer. Various issues.

Pilot (Journal of the National Insurance Association). Various issues.

INDEX

Italic page numbers refer to illustrations.

ROBERT E. WEEMS, JR., is Assistant Professor of History at the University of Missouri–Columbia.